THE
SACRED
VISION

THE

SACRED
VISION

NATIVE AMERICAN RELIGION
AND ITS PRACTICE TODAY

Michael F. Steltenkamp

PAULIST PRESS
New York/Ramsey

ACKNOWLEDGMENTS

Grateful acknowledgment is made to the sources cited in the bibliography and footnotes for permission to reprint quotations in this text. A special word of thanks is also extended to the Jesuits of South Dakota's Pine Ridge and Rosebud Reservations, especially Paul Steinmetz, S.J. The *Jesuit Council for Theological Reflection* not only provided financial assistance, but also encouragement for this project. Reverend Mr. Ted Yadivisiak and his wife Dorothy from the Diocesan Order of Women provided their home as my base-of-contact with the Northern Ontario Ojibwa, and their support enabled this book to be completed. Similarly, Mary Ayers typed the work's many drafts. And, finally, the inspiration of this writing came from Indian people themselves, and their influence upon me I consider heaven-sent.

Copyright © 1982 by
Michael Steltenkamp

Library of Congress
Catalog Card Number 82-60594

ISBN: 0-8091-2481-5

Published by Paulist Press
545 Island Road, Ramsey, N.J. 07446

Printed and bound in the
United States of America

Contents

To the memory of nine Lakota youth—whose short time on earth might still "help us to remember that all the fruits of the wingeds, the two-leggeds, and the four-leggeds, are really the gifts of *Wakan-Tanka*. They are all *wakan* and should be treated as such!"

—*The Sacred Pipe*

PROLOGUE

The doctor said to the Bishop, "So you see, my lord, your young ordinand can live no more than three years and doesn't know it. Will you tell him, and what will you do with him?"

The Bishop said to the doctor, "Yes, I'll tell him, but not yet. If I tell him now, he'll try too hard. How much time has he for an active life?"

"A little less than two years if he's lucky."

"So short a time to learn so much? It leaves me no choice. I shall send him to my hardest parish. I shall send him to Kingcome on patrol of the Indian villages."

"Then I hope you'll pray for him, my lord."

But the Bishop only answered gently that it was where he would wish to go if he were young again, and in the ordinand's place.

1

This introduction to Margaret Craven's *I Heard the Owl Call My Name* is striking. Interest is immediately teased by the author's delicate handling of such important human concerns as faith, reason, hope, despair, life, death, the best of times and worst. A newly-ordained priest is diagnosed as having a terminal illness. His good and wise superior then instinctively decides that a remote Indian tribe would be the young man's best instructor for passage to eternity. As the story progresses, readers learn to agree with the Bishop's pastoral sensitivity. They learn to see that Indian people do indeed have something special, something holy, something divine *and* intimately wedded to real-life concerns.

John Collier, one-time Commissioner of Indian Affairs, suggested in more direct terms why Native America was important for people to consider. He wrote:

> They had what the world has lost. They have it now. What the world has lost, the world must have again, lest it die. Not many years are left to have or have not, to recapture the lost ingredient ... the power to live. ...

This captivating, but vague, literary lifeline was rooted in the Commissioner's substantial contact with many Indian groups. To his credit, Collier convinced many people that Native traditions offered avenues of relief from the anxieties of modern life. Collier heard within Native traditions a voice that calmed inner ferment, a voice that encouraged self-affirmation, a voice that promised a hopeful destiny.

Craven and Collier eloquently addressed a complex of spiritual wrestlings. They did this through a people whose identity has often been locked within a realm of mystery and shadow. Historically, such distancing has created either a genocidal posture toward Indians, or a mentality almost deifying their imagined attributes. The former has bred racism, while the latter has incarnated the bubblings of Ponce De Leon's mythical fountain of youth. Somewhere between these extremes lies the reality of flesh-and-blood Native America.

2

Countless seekers of a spiritual vision enter Indian territory. Frequently, they desire to establish ties with some respected elder who might initiate them into the mystery of Native religion. Such a tack usually meets with little, if any, success. Others anxiously await the publication of each new book dealing with Indians—having been reared on the romantic yarns of James Fenimore Cooper, and nurtured by classics like *Black Elk Speaks, A Century of Dishonor,* and the Curtis photograph collection.

So well read are some persons that they become walking libraries of Indian legend and lore. For example, a member of the Sioux tribe visited Germany one summer and returned to tell his friends: "They knew more about Indians than I did." As is the case in several European countries, Germany has pockets of people bound together through their common interest in Indian life. Their Sioux visitor was amazed to see an imitation of his people's traditional lifestyle, but it bore little resemblance to the reservation existence he had temporarily left behind. He appreciated the obvious show of respect, but knew that more than an ocean separated their cultures. Nonetheless, a strange appeal from Native America continues to allure individuals searching for a spiritual commodity the Indian religious system, however vaguely understood, seems to offer.

Urban sprawl, frenetic rush-hours, monotonous daily routines synchronized to a ticking mechanism on every wrist, all stand in stark contrast to a way of life appearing more at ease with itself, more in union with cosmic forces, and more at peace with the limitations of being human. Indeed, people might honestly question the assets and liabilities of a "Christian" culture that foreigners often label as "ugly American." Indian spirituality is seen as perhaps offering a viable alternative during a period of confusion or rootlessness, and Native people themselves have joined this re-evaluation. A kind of exodus has begun toward the promised land of Indian religious practice.

3

Much ethnographic literature exists which accurately sketches Native life, past and present. For years, social scientists have earned abiding reputations within scholarly circles for the important studies of Indian America which they produced for the academic community. And in recent times, Native people themselves have entered the public forum to express opinions they deem most relevant to their culture's existence. But all commentators, be they Indian or not, are forever confronted with the task of interpreting such extensive data with a most discriminating eye.

Often the vivifying spirit which sustains a tribe's ceremonialism is hidden behind a vocabulary known only to university professors. Contrasting with this are the fanciful musings of drawing-room romantics. Their prose conjures up beautiful Native princesses and noble Indian knights from a land which only exists in dreamy imaginations. Again, between these extremes rests the lived-experience of culturally diverse people whose pilgrimage through life might truly illumine the path trod by questing others. Native America might extend a vision to those outside its boundary, but in order to find it people must be willing to tackle an enormous amount of material.

If one seeks adventure, Indian history can match the likes of Hannibal, Cleopatra, and many illustrious others. It can likewise chronicle the sad and tragic. The theoretically inclined, on the other hand, can look to a small tribe and probably postulate some universal truth from the study of a little-known fertility rite. But pre-determined expectations can make Indian-life a grab-bag of unlimited wish-fulfillment (often bearing little resemblance to anything particularly vital today). Barring this whimsical tendency in favor of an honest effort to understand, one can expect to find a challenge in the manifestations of Native spirituality. God's voice can certainly be heard, but can a person listen with the sensitivity or openness required?

In light of the above tendencies, it is clear that misinformation abounds. Hence, one should exercise caution before dispatching the more familiar forms of religious practice and espousing some new creed. An individual ought to know that this disarray exists. Then, one can more wisely investigate what Indian religion is. So what is it?

The variety of approaches to the study of Native Spirituality is great, so the answer to such a question might be endlessly pursued. One writer has recently observed that much has been written about Indian religion, but most of it has failed to effectively translate Native religious experience for non-participants. Consequently, this book proposes a route of entry for readers seeking direction, for persons who are drawn to experience God's revelation among a people different than their own.

This book will focus on religious practices and attitudes which are presently found (to varying degrees) in many tribes across the country. It is hoped that this excursion into the Native world will justly reverence Indian spiritual tradition, and perhaps illumine shadowy lifepaths which at times loom so threatening.

Throughout these pages, the terms "Native" and "Indian" will be used interchangeably when referring to America's first inhabitants. Some would object to this, and not without reason. However, their use here is not intended to reveal any kind of social or political statement. Rather, they are employed colloquially by non-Indian and Native people today and, so, are simply convenient.

In recent years, groups have reverted to calling themselves by their original "Indian language" name (even when given individuals are not fluent in their ancestral tongue). A non-Indian might, for example, live in "Chippewa" country for years, and now start to hear people saying: "We are *Anishnabe.*" Similarly, western "Sioux" have been famous the world over, but few would associate them with "*Lakota.*" From the beginning of European contact, Native America has been labeled with misunderstanding that only in recent times has been effectively resisted. This present-day "name" controversy is just one case in point.

Thinking he had found a western route to India, Columbus presumed that he met "Indians." Later colonists met eastern groups who daubed on red grease for protection against the weather, and so we had "The Red Man." America's Native population, rich in varied lifestyles and languages, greeted the new immigrants and were both amazed and mortified. They were unprepared for the challenges to come.

As is now generally known, the interface of European and Native cultures bred bilateral conflict and confusion.

The privilege of hindsight allows us to see mistakes in the past, mourn, and then try to keep them buried. This book is an effort to do just that. It is an excursion into the lived-experience of religious people, a face-to-face portrayal of human beings in search of what Western scholarship calls "the Supernatural." Theoretical considerations, though present, will remain more implicit than drawn out, and this method has been chosen because there has been a "rapid growth in the amount of trivia being published in ... learned journals ... more and more about less and less."[1] In fact, the present literature by or about Native America often winds up becoming overly academic or rhetorical. As this pattern affects religion, the former becomes lost to the general public and the latter inflames impressionable minds without offering coherent direction.

Indian religious practice will be shown as a prophetic challenge to spiritual complacency. Where credibly lived, it clearly tempers the religious ethnocentrism of other peoples. By the same token, some Native readers will be moved to confront very vital issues that prevail today. As pride in tradition is reawakened, as "roots" or religious consciousness is tapped, integrity glows or fades in proportion to a creed's enfleshment. Pan-Indian revitalization efforts have spawned ad lib rituals, and lip-service to Native religion has captured earnest inquirers. Indian people have thus been caught in the very difficult position of reordering their lifestyle in a more holistic way, or settling for a vacuous, flag-waving nationalism.

In their 1977 letter to Native America, the Catholic bishops acknowledged the Church's indebtedness to Indi-

1. Marvin Harris, *The Rise of Anthropological Theory*, Harper & Row, New York, 1968.

an people for witnessing to faith in God through years of oppression. Furthermore, the bishops recognized that Native America's struggle for religious identity was not unique. It is a vocation shared by everyone, a matter of life and death, and at the core of human meaning. Church leaders stated that increased dialogue in our common search for truth is the only path to take. And this book is a step toward that Life which God offers us all.

INTRODUCTION

For over a dozen years, much of my enrichment has come through studying about or involving myself with Native American people—a relatively short journey compared with some of my Jesuit brothers, scholars, and other individuals affected by Native American life. On the other hand, a blessing of events and persons has kindled a type of inner flame which disposes me to share its cumulative light with fellow-travelers who were simply at a different point and a different time along the way.

Avoiding dogmatic claims, I offer only reflections here which are meant to be interesting at least, and instructive for personal decision at best. Most people struggle with religious faith, or meaning, at some point in their lives, and try to resolve the tension in one way or another. This work will perhaps be of special help to the spiritually restless children of God who find themselves torn between choices, and who figuratively flip a coin while praying that gravity be non-existent.

Although not technically a manual for religious discernment, the text I write may help such a process—even though some inherent biases might seem to exist. My words are those of a man, but woman continues to give me life in varieties of human encounter. My formal education is extensive, but the uneducated have taught me much. A great deal of this work will stem from experience with a few tribes, but its spirit is more universal. Racially, I am non-Indian, but my heart is bonded to Native concerns. And I carry the title of Catholic priest, even though many persons young and old, male and female, have shown me the faces of minister I can only pray to someday possess.

Prior to much extended contact with reservation life, I undertook graduate studies. During this period, I was a student of Harold Driver—a scholar of some magnitude regarding Indian life. Using his own work, *Indians of North America* (a standard reference in the field), Driver instilled in us a keen appreciation for the diverse cultures found within Indian country. He was available for conferences outside of class, and on many occasions we discussed matters pertaining to the Indian world.

I was likewise fortunate to participate in a course offered by Joseph Epes Brown—a visiting professor known primarily for his work with the famous Sioux holy man, Black Elk. Brown's topic for the semester was "Religious Traditions of Native North America," and his class was well attended. Among the many lectures he presented, the most captivating for me dealt with his experience of spiritual sonship to Black Elk—their interaction harvesting *The Sacred Pipe,* a delicate and moving account about the seven sacred rites of the Sioux.

As with Driver, Brown and I exchanged reflections many times—our common ground being that I was going to teach on the very reservation where he and Black Elk once lived. Brown wished me well when we parted. He knew of my eagerness to find life's "lost ingredient"—alluded to by Collier and said to be retained by persons such as Black Elk. Upon leaving school, I harbored a desire to find the holy man's son, Ben, and perhaps accomplish for him what Neihardt did for his father in the decades-old but ever-new *Black Elk Speaks.*

Shortly after my arrival on the Pine Ridge Reservation in South Dakota, I met the aging Benjamin Black Elk. Teaching Native American Studies and being involved with other activities among the Sioux high school students prevented me from seeing Ben until a year later. He died shortly thereafter, just a couple of weeks prior to 1973's internationally publicized, militant takeover of Wounded Knee—a small reservation settlement located near the historic encounter between well-armed troops and an already-defeated band of Sioux in 1890. Most of the latter group today lie buried on a hill at the crossroads of Wounded Knee.

Black Elk is said to have once reflected that his people's "dream" died in the bloody snows of Wounded Knee—Ben's death at the time of Wounded Knee II signaling for me the demise of a personal hope. Unfortunately, a visitor at Pine Ridge today might well be inclined to affirm the holy man's sad reflection about his people—a malaise of spirit too often evident and social-spiritual diseases too prevalent. Nine of my student-friends, for instance, died violently and needlessly within the span of four years—fresh, young faces and bright minds snuffed out from a school of less than two hundred! Romantic notions about Indian life I entertained during my pre-reservation days had little staying-power once I tearfully observed that the chilling reality of mere survival was often at stake.

But as much as one can say about the rampant ills infecting Native America, prolonged contact with Indian people discloses (sometimes very clearly, sometimes in glimpses) a spiritual resilience and human vitality which surely prevented genocide from becoming an accom-

plished fact. Not long after the Wounded Knee occupa-
tion, these elusive qualities, this "lost ingredient,"
became something very much a part of my experience
through extended contact with Black Elk's only surviving
child, Lucy—a grandmother I met while seated on a
bench one ordinary, but special, spring day. From that
time on, I became a regular visitor at her family's remote-
ly situated loghouse.

I learned, however, that the presence of Jesuits at
Black Elk's home was actually part of a seventy-year tradition started long ago when the "old religion" holy man
first became a Catholic catechist among his people. The
valuable contributions of Neihardt and Brown to the legacy of Indian tradition reported only part of the holy
man's religious journey. And so, in deference to Lucy's
long-desired "vision," I put down in writing the comple-
tion of her father's life-story.

All of the above, though, is prelude to the more universal concerns this text is intended to address. As stated
earlier, Native America has projected (correctly or not) a
spiritual integrity many persons wish to possess, and perhaps even acquire by means of the same vehicles of expression. Black Elk of the Sioux has, over the course of
many years, surfaced as a most eminent spokesperson on
behalf of Native religion. His commentaries which spell
out the use of the Sacred Pipe, and his recollections of a
time no more, profoundly touch the hearts of all who read
his work.

Having been with the holy man's family sharing
their most intimate spiritual concerns, and having participated in Native religious practices, I believe what Collier
referred to as "lost" from most of humankind is, in fact,
within our reach. The "power to live" anew might be fur-
thered by reflection on what I shall suggest are central

themes of Native spirituality. The "power to live" is within reach if we can somehow find the way to open our hands and grasp its seemingly ever-offered Presence.

For example, people with strong religious convictions have always been a part of history. In many cultures a God was perceived as speaking, appropriately enough, in words peculiar to varying environments. Spiritually conscious persons lived beyond the convenient category of being "ecumenical" or "superstitious" and simply took for granted what so many others have found worthy of debate. That is, tradition-bearers of the Indian world frequently appear quite accommodating to new understandings of God, while their non-Indian counterparts often remain quite aloof or parochial, agnostic or atheistic.

Contemporary Christian theology does not regard God's historical enfleshment through Jesus as a testimony to divine silence outside the greater Mediterranean area. Rather, God is recognized as so loving the world that he took visible, flesh-and-blood form in Jesus and thus personally embraced a human existence he *at all times and in all places* cherished very deeply. As will be seen, however, this modern, personalistic understanding of "God" could almost be called "traditional" among many different Indian societies.

Having been reared on sacred stories of their own, Native peoples gave rather ready assent upon hearing biblical tales, and then, in turn, explained what was sacred in their tradition. One such special story of divine revelation dealt with the giving of the Sacred Pipe—consideration of which is essential for tapping the life-blood of Indian spirituality.

Part One of this book will explore the Pipe's lived-meaning among one representative group. Part Two will then address the Native American Church—a more re-

cent, highly ceremonial, religious movement that has ex-
plicitly blended biblical themes with Indian traditions.
These pan-Indian phenomena are the foundation of Part
Three—an exposé of spiritual sentiments that are not unlike the theology mentioned above. This last section
shows that, over time, God has indeed spoken to different
cultures. Investigating this revelation should certainly be,
as Scripture reports, "good news."

PART ONE

The Sacred Pipe
of the Sioux

Early one morning, long ago, two young men decided to leave their village and go out hunting. They journeyed far from camp in search of game. Meeting with success, they started back. Standing on a hill, they looked to the horizon and saw something coming toward them which, upon drawing near, turned out to be a beautiful maiden dressed in white buckskin. She was carrying a bundle in her arms—perhaps a child. It was difficult to see, but her beauty was not. Desire grew within the men, as they saw just how lovely she was.

Wishing to satisfy his urges, one of the hunters decided to molest the girl. He said to his companion: "No one is near. We can lie with her for pleasure, and no one can stop us." Such were the thoughts of the one man. But his friend responded: "What you have said is wrong to do! This woman looks to be special, her beauty mysterious, her bearing sacred!" At this point of their conversation, the maiden stood directly in front of them and said: "I have heard you speaking. I do not wish to have any trouble with you because I am on a mission from God." Hearing that, the

21

man with evil designs said to his friend: "We can easily get her now, and do as we wish. Her voice kindles my desire even more!" But the companion replied: "I can have no part in your plan, but I shall not stop you." The girl placed the bundle she was carrying on the ground, and faced her attacker.

Going ahead with his plot, the man of bad intentions moved forward and forced the maiden downward. Just as he was about to be satisfied, thunder could be heard in the heavens. A cloud descended and enveloped the pair—the other hunter standing terrified as he watched this scene unfold. In but a few moments, the cloud lifted and revealed the beautiful maiden, untouched, once again holding her bundle and standing in front of the onlooker. At her feet was the lustful hunter's skeleton—snakes crawling out of it.

Upon seeing all of this, the frightened hunter began an abrupt departure from the spot, but was halted by the maiden's statement: "Do not be afraid! Listen well to what I am about to say." The soothing tone of the girl's voice was as beautiful to hear as her appearance was to behold, so the man lingered and listened. His earlier suspicion was confirmed. This was indeed a person lovely to be near, to gaze upon, and certainly respect. The mysterious, beautiful one spoke: "Go back to your village and have the people prepare a lodge for my arrival. I am bringing something which will be of great value to them, which will make them happy, and be their means of prayer and union with God."

The hunter hastened back to his village and informed the leader and his people of all that had happened. The village did as he instructed— prepared a special lodge, and prepared their hearts to welcome this sacred visitor. Shortly after they had completed his instructions, the beautiful lady came among them and presented her gift wrapped in the bundle—a gift from heaven, the sacred pipe. She told them how to use the pipe, how to pray with it, and she stated that in the course of time seven rites would be revealed to the tribe. These were to be performed so that the people might live, and have life in abundance. The sacred pipe would be key to the performance of these holy rites, as it embodied the lesson that "all are relatives" under God. Its use would insure preservation of this insight, and help the people walk the road of good and not falter.

When the lovely maiden departed, she was transformed into a buffalo calf—eventually disappearing over a nearby hill. This is why the pipe is sometimes called the "sacred calf pipe." The people knew that they had received a special blessing this day, cherishing fulfillment of the beautiful maiden's heavenly promise.

As strange as the above story may sound to moderns, it makes up (along with other narratives not included here) part of what might be considered the ancient-Sioux equivalent to Judaeo-Christian Scripture. And although the account reported belongs to the oral religious tradition of the Sioux, other tribes possess stories invested with profound, sacred imperatives very comparable to those originating with the beautiful maiden's appearance.

At one time or another, in fact, all of Native America made use of pipes either for religious functions or for purposes of leisure. Different areas of the country maintained one emphasis or the other. For example, a scholar with many years of experience among different tribes stated that the full depth of Plains Indian religion might *only* be understood through study of the pipe and its accompanying ritual. Likewise, many groups east of the Mississippi accorded the pipe a central role while southwestern peoples, by contrast, developed other religious ceremonies with less emphasis on it. Today, however, a good number of Indian people from coast to coast recognize and promote the pipe as a spiritual symbol common to their heritage. It has become somewhat of a religious thread binding the many-patterned fabric of Indian culture and religion.

Yet, because social deterioration has fragmented so many tribes and slain their traditions of old, Indian regard for the pipe has often been reduced to that of the ordinary citizen's. One's knowledge or ignorance is largely fashioned by mass-media presentations which are frequently misleading, fictitious, or shallow. But despite this infertile ground of social existence, roots of the Indian heritage still cling to the pipe as an eminently important source of identity nourishment. Such is why, for instance, a rural Abenaki from the east can meet with a reservation Shoshone from Wyoming and urban Chippewa from St. Paul—and celebrate their solidarity through smoking of this unique, ritual instrument. Their action, though, is not something foreign to Western tradition. The Christian's breaking of bread is analogous to this centuries-old

Indian practice. In both rituals, transcendence is perceived to operate and bind.

Briefly stated, of the many and diverse forms which
make up Native American spiritual practice, the pipe
emerges as a recurrent symbol of religious expression. It
is not the totality of Indian religion, nor a tool which syn-
thesizes the creed of any one tribe. It is, however, a commonly recognized instrument of ritual overarching the
North American continent. Hence, the pipe is a necessary
focal point for the eyes of spiritually inquisitive people.

My knowledge of the pipe was first dependent upon
study associated with various graduate school projects.
Research was the order of the day as I consulted the work
of distinguished ethnographers. In addition to them, I .
noted that members of the Lewis and Clark expedition
regularly saw rituals in which the pipe was used, as did
George Catlin after them (even sketching pictures of different pipes he observed). My ubiquitous and revered
brother Jesuit of the last century, Pierre DeSmet, also
contributed extensive commentaries pertaining to Indian
life as a whole and the "calumet" in particular (a French-
Canadian reference to the pipe). It presided, he wrote, at
all feasts and ceremonies—regardless of their political,
religious, or social nature.

Motivated, too, by sheer interest in Native religious
practice, I gleaned from Bureau of Ethnology reports a
large number of citations dealing with usage of the pipe.
Such material is certainly important for anyone inclined
to tackle a specialized research project. But rather than
restate the findings of anthropology students, I prefer to
address the lived-experience of pipe spirituality as I encountered it. Far from the closed recesses of a university
library, the idea of pipe became for me a concrete reality.
It was not a quaint object of speculation among people

with whom I worked (tribes of the Plains and woodlands) but was a living tradition preserved from of old.

What I generally report in these reflections, then, is the reconciliation between theory and practice (always, it seems, one of life's ongoing challenges). My goal is to balance the many conceptions of Native religious traditions which have been lopsidedly directed at one pole or the other. The "power to live" might be more accessible through such a presentation.

The Use of the Sacred Pipe Today

Pipes were used in any number of ceremonies during my days at Pine Ridge, and their appearance always dictated a certain hushed attention. Those who were not comfortable in seeing the pipe used (for one reason or another) still knew that its employment was not to be outwardly challenged. And thus a careful silence always characterized the age-old drama of performing what the Buffalo Maiden had instructed.

This corporate sense of reverence is rooted, however, in what seems to be a gift common to most Indian people—belief in God![1] And such faith (it appeared to me) was usually tolerant of any particular religious gathering (be it involved with the pipe or not). For instance, I often participated at Mass with Indians, and was edified by their obvious embrace of Christianity. But closer inquiry revealed a spectrum of belief.

---

1. Phrases like *Kitchi Manitou, Wakan Tanka,* and others are traditional designations for the highest Supernatural Power. Commonly translated "Great Spirit," the reference is as conventional to modern Indians as the term "God" is to Westerners. Parallel understandings and mystifications likewise obtain. Qualifications are often required as to past and present monotheistic or animistic notions, but these do not fall within the scope of considerations here.

One person might say: "We are Catholics and do not use pagan expressions such as the pipe." Another might say: "We are Catholics and we integrate our older tradition (of the pipe) with our newer practice." Still another will decalre: "I am Catholic and Indian! I follow the two traditions separately because they cannot be one." The gamut of lived-opinion was not complete until I encountered people who were physically present at Mass, but who simply could not affiliate their hearts with anything but the pipe practice (or none at all). Nonetheless, be a ceremony that of the pipe ritual or the Mass, a deep spiritual sense (common to most Indian people) made solemnity the order of the day.

As with custodians of the older tradition, "medicine men" might surprise the casual visitor to Indian country by claiming membership in some Christian denomination.[2] Others might reveal a two-track mentality which simply views the traditions as separate but equal. And then, some will militantly eschew any identification with Christianity. This latter group has begun to assert itself more vigorously in recent years where before an individual was commonly known as either a Catholic or a Protestant medicine man! Thus, to generalize about Indian religious practice is difficult because of such ongoing historical conditions. Even so, whatever denominational or

2. Within Native North America, social organization reveals what commentators have called the band, tribe, chiefdom, and state. Similarly, religious practice included private revelations, visionaries with followers, herbal and ritual specialists (men and women), and hereditary priesthoods. This text will not belabor these distinctions (granted their importance for cultural studies). Instead, terms used in everyday parlance among Indian people will be employed so as to maintain focus on the context reported. "Medicine man" (derived from the French *médicin,* doctor) traditionally referred to men or women who possessed some kind of curative power. Today, however, it commonly refers to anyone specializing in ceremonies perceived by a group as traditional.

non-denominational religious involvement a pipe-user might claim (however complete or partially practiced), the important issue is that such a person would simply be regarded as more or less devout in one or two traditions.

The basic ritual is easily enough described. First the pipe stem is pointed toward the four cardinal directions—beginning (among the Sioux) westward, then to the north, east, south, then skyward, and finally to the earth. A pinch of tobacco is placed in the bowl accompanied by prayers with each gesture (if the bowl has not been filled prior to the offering). Contrary to what marijuana advocates might want to hear, smoking material usually consisted of tobacco mixed with a variety of tree barks.[3]

The stem common to ceremonial use varies, but is generally one to two feet in length. Some have decorative incising (for instance, a turtle form). Others have none. Bowls are usually made of the red catlinite which tourists see quarried at Pipestone National Monument in Minnesota, but some bowls are also yellowish or black in color. Sometimes the figure of an animal is carved on the stone (e.g., a buffalo), while others are smooth and plain. Other adornments can also be found on pipes, their meaning associated with the owner's personal vision or tribe's treasury of myth and legend.

Prayer content during this ritual varies according to the occasion, and occasions are likewise diverse. Someone might pray with the pipe at a high school graduation, a funeral, the installation of tribal officers, traditional ceremonies conducted by medicine men, or alone on a hill—away from distraction—seeking God's will. Consequently, one using the pipe speaks prayers appropriate to

---

3. Interestingly, tobacco was consumed, rather than smoked, in some areas.

the situation—inspiration and spontaneity characterizing
the different spiritual moments.

At first glance, the pipe might appear to be of second-
ary importance during ceremonies. It may, for instance,
be overshadowed by other ritual practices (such as singing, body movement, praying, etc.) and capture a group's
attention for but a short period of time. Here again the
analogy of the Christian Eucharist might obtain. Partak-
ing of the consecrated bread or wine might occur, for example, within very simple or very elaborate liturgical
settings. Singing, dancing, praying, incensing, reading,
preaching, and other creative expressions of spirituality
may or may not take place at different eucharistic gatherings. Good Friday services dramatically ritualize the dark
sadness of Calvary, while Easter then jubilantly cele-
brates the bright hope of the risen Lord. Within each context, however, the bread or cup is shared and is central to
the community's faith-life. So, too, the pipe is passed
among participants in similarly varied Indian rituals.

The summer of 1977 witnessed two southwestern
tribes signing a treaty and celebrating the end of a centuries-old feud. Elsewhere, a wing of Chicago's prestigious
Art Museum saw medicine men pray at the opening of an
exhibition which featured Indian life. Meanwhile, a
friend of mine in Pine Ridge convened a four-night healing ceremony within the darkened confines of his rural
cabin. At each occasion, the pipe was instrumental in defining the purpose of gathering together.

Burning twists of sweetgrass or pieces of cedar-
branch serve as a type of incense, with body movement
and "rubrics" executed with a finesse Christian liturgists
would do well to imitate. Incensing the group gathered,
the sacred area, the pipe, and one's self precedes the actual offering of the pipe—the performance not only being

reverent but also engagingly hypnotic. Persons who conduct such ceremonies are, more often than not, quite
adept at commanding the attention of all present. So
when the pipe is to be used, people know something sacred and special is about to occur. The divine is perceived
to be drawing near, and silence enables one's listening for
the approach.

But lest the impression being given here is one of oth-
er-worldly strangeness and mystical silence as necessary
backdrop to pipe usage, a digression may be in order so as
to best reveal the human participants who are involved
with such rituals.

One night I participated in a ceremony which consisted of praying for someone who had recently left the
community. Although much effort was expended on
preparation for the special prayer service, more seemed
to be directed at the "feed" which would follow. Several
women were busily attending to kitchen duties while
men stood leisurely awaiting the religious activity that
would precede eating time.

When I had arrived early in the evening, an old dog
was moving suspiciously around the loghouse porch—
prompting me to wonder if one of its young was to be the
special food served later on. As time passed and as activities increased, I forgot about the dog (which had disappeared anyway) and attended to friendly visiting. All the
time, women were brewing and boiling and organizing
dinnerware for what everyone eagerly anticipated—a
good meal after a good spiritual observance.

The medicine man conducted about an hour-long ceremony (in total darkness) where blessings were asked for
the person who had gone away. Individuals petitioned
God's help for different problems of life. At the ceremony's conclusion, lights were turned on and several women

immediately exited to bring on the tasty morsels everyone looked forward to having.

We were all seated on the floor, forming a haphazard circle—I being next to a grandmother whose muscular frame was regarded as an asset against cold nights and heavy work. The serving women came to us one after another and poured coffee, passed bread, and dished out stew. Just as I was wondering what we were being served, my matronly neighbor exclaimed: "I'll take that old dog's tail—nobody else wants it!" In the process of scooping, a strangely familiar canine tail had fallen to the floor and grandmother seized the opportunity to provoke fits of laughter from everyone. The dog I observed earlier in the evening had indeed good reason to be suspicious! For the rest of our time together, light conversation was humorously interrupted by someone referring to grandmother's unconventional appetite.[4]

This example is simply intended to illustrate that when the pipe is used, it serves as a punctuating focal point of prayer. When this purpose is fulfilled, people assume a very casual posture with as much or as little reference to the ceremony as they like. There need be no lingering aura of mystery.

Even though rote prayers are not the custom and a "systematic theology" of the pipe varies with each practioner, some commonly held themes are recognizable. When, for example, the pipe is lifted toward the different directions, the powers of the universe are being entreated. The wooden stem represents all flora, animal designs all fauna, and appended feathers all that fly. The tobacco

---

4. Years ago, eating dogmeat was common among many tribes and avoided by others. Today its consumption is generally reserved for traditional rites such as the one reported here. Its taste reminded me of turkey.

grains represent the multiple creatures born of God, and so all space and all creation is brought into play through the pipe ritual. Submission to and dependence upon God is articulated by the presider on behalf of everyone present. Voices of faith are raised in prayer, assured by the Sacred Lady that their hearts will be heard.

This description of religious practice is not an observable reality day-in-and-day-out. Use of the pipe is reserved for only special public or personal events. A visitor to any reservation could spend several weeks, months, or longer within Indian country and leave convinced that the ancient practice is simply non-existent. The fact is, however, that the Sacred Lady's "child" is alive and well (even if somewhat hidden from view).

In times long past, replicas fashioned after the original pipe were a very visible sign of Native practice. Most every adult possessed one. But the commingling of other Indian and non-Indian religious traditions has marginalized the pipe's undisputed claim to primacy. The social ferment of a century has, likewise, accosted the religious spirit of Native people and tarnished what was once a prevailing spiritual fervor. Nevertheless, so strong was the pipe tradition at one time that most people are still at least cautious in relation to it. And some (generically referred to as "medicine men") have preserved its legacy. Anonymous other men and women pray with the pipe in the quiet of their homes.

In recent years, anger has been expressed that regular smoking of the pipe was intended for only those who had made the "vision quest." This "quest" (a sacred rite itself) is the secluded confinement of an individual upon a hill for several days—time set aside as in a Christian "retreat." A medicine man is usually asked to oversee the individual's preparation for and placement on a designated piece of ground—the sacred space wherein the divine reveals a guiding "vision" to follow during life. A sweatlodge ceremony (discussed later on) precedes and concludes this two to four day experience. Without first undertaking this quest (or "pipe fast" as it is also called) an individual has no right to pray with the pipe—so some would claim.[5]

Perhaps because of the menstrual taboo, women were kept at a distance from pipe ceremonies. But this prohibition, though still strongly in effect in some areas, has weakened considerably. Participation of women in the vision quest, sweatlodge, and other accompanying rituals is now not uncommon.

Woman's mysterious, monthly flow was a sacred event—a defining mark that separated the sexes. Hence, segregation was required for reverence of such a gift. However, contemporary influences from the dominant cultures are strong. Mixing of the sexes often occurs with little, if any, attention paid to menstrual injunctions. In some respects, the restrictive nature of this widespread phenomenon was a kind of religious salute to procreation's necessary opposites. Instead of being negative, it seems more a religious expression of *Vive la différence!*

As far as who can or cannot smoke a pipe, local custom might be the only "rule of thumb" to go by. A Chippewa medicine man explained to me that healers alone could use black-bowl pipes. Holy-men were entrusted with grey-bowl pipes. And all could smoke from those carved out of red stone. I asked why women were not permitted access to the grey or black, to which he simply responded: "It's not our tradition." Anthropologist Ruth

5. In August 1980 death occurred during a vision quest in California. The suppliant was a diabetic who neglected to take his medicine.

Underhill asked similar questions in the southwest and received the common answer: ". . . we have always done it that way."[6]

On the other hand, a reservation patriarch (whose lineage is revered and authoritative) explained to me that the pipe was like Christ. He said that "just as Christ was for all people, so is the pipe." As if aware of the counter-arguments I was contemplating while he spoke, the grandfather's ninety-year-old face wrinkled insistently as he continued: "You don't have to get any great vision! You use the pipe to pray with, to speak to God—young and old, man and woman. Anybody can pray with the pipe, and should! That's why God gave it to us." Nevertheless, within Indian country differing perspectives continue to be expressed. Meanwhile, the pipe is smoked and prayers are made—some lives clearly reflecting spiritual integrity, others seeming to be little more than masquerade (another, this time unfortunate, parallel to Christian practice).

Stories about the pipe's "power" are legion. If the folklore is accurate, spectacular and extraordinary supernatural events are not restricted to only Fatima and Lourdes. For example, one repeatedly hears about the pipe's control of weather. If a storm is desired, people are known who have prayed with the pipe to make it come. If a storm is feared, the pipe can make it go away. And if one is praying with the pipe on a hill when rain comes, no drops sprinkle on that particular area.

Among the Sioux, sacred myth underwrites this pipe/thunderstorm relationship. A manifestation of God-head is the thunderbird of the west—protector of the pipe, whose glance is lightning (which, like the pipe, "con-

6. Quoted in *Red Man's Religion*, p. 247.

nects" heaven and earth). Anyone tempted to abuse the
pipe or its ritual hesitates in fear of a death-dealing repri-
sal. A story circulates that people once stole the original
pipe from its keeper and were later found dead. Lightning dealt their demise and the pipe was mysteriously returned. Thus, the presence of an eagle on high (always a
good omen, but seldom seen) is especially significant during the ceremonies involving the pipe. Some think it
might just be a sign of the thunderbird's heavenly, protec-
tive presence.

Questing for a Vision of the Sacred Pipe

With the cultural resurgence of Native America these
past years, non-Indians in general and non-Native
church people in particular have sometimes found themselves unwelcome at ceremonies rooted in the old religious practice. If one's personal spirituality was known to
be deep, then interaction was possible because approaching God was recognized as transcultural. Nonetheless,
where formerly there existed a rather open acceptance of
non-Indian participation, social pressure has been clos-
ing off access.

Because of these social dynamics, my opportunity to
be significantly involved with Native religion seemed
less and less a realizable goal. Pressures from the Indian
"left" were becoming simply too much to contend with by
the old-time practitioners. It was increasingly difficult to
even request information as respondents tended to be
evasive. Those willing to speak were usually ill-informed.
And so, my dream of ever seeing the original sacred pipe,
the one popularly thought of as given by the maiden, appeared byond the realm of possibility.

For years, the Cheyenne River Reservation of central

South Dakota has been the place where the original pipe was kept. Indians from around the country who seek a major source of the pipe tradition look to that country with reverence—as the Siouan myth is perhaps the best known. But unlike the monument motif of Western civilization, the pipe's environment is a small, out-of-the-way community called Green Grass. No markers indicate anything special preserved in this remote village (located twenty miles from Eagle Butte, the reservation's main town), and most local people seem to pay little attention to those who conduct the pipe rituals. In short, only oral tradition (which modern Indians sometimes call the "moccasin telegraph") circulates news pertinent to people concerned about pipe activities.

On July 13, 1976, the "telegraph" was in operation carrying my name and that of a fellow Jesuit. My colleague had established ties with a one-time resident of Cheyenne River who agreed to take us on a "pilgrimage" to Green Grass. Our Indian guide (whom I shall refer to as Lame Foot) was a traditionalist with long-standing friendship to the Catholic "Blackrobes." He had been brought up a Catholic near Green Grass prior to taking a wife and raising his family on the Pine Ridge Reservation. Knowing our intentions were grounded on religious concern, Lame Foot assumed the responsibility of introducing us to the pipe's keeper and pleading our case.

Since every pipe used is endowed with the power of the maiden's pipe, people need never make the long trek to Green Grass. And yet, visiting this special place is always entertained by those deeply involved with spiritual matters. Most medicine men have made this trip, but other people simply venerate their tradition by practicing the rites from afar.

When we left that morning for Eagle Butte, I harbored hopes and doubts. By the day's end would I see the pipe keeper, the pipe, and the Jerusalem or Mecca of Indian religious tradition? Or would I have traveled a couple hundred miles only to be turned away (if not spurned)? After all, anti-Christian militants had expressed little compatibility with what we represented.

The modern Indian scene (perhaps the world in general, too) is often a testimony to what might be called "experimental religion." People search for a spiritual identity and abandon older ones that do not produce some kind of instant gratification. Christianity had at one time been accepted, as in non-Indian America, but social trends were making it unfashionable. Apart from representing a religion that no longer "worked," we were racially identified as the cause of oppression.

Lame Foot had not been to the Green Grass community for some time, and we were not even sure the keeper would be home. The outcome of our journey was tenuous at best. We were taking a leap of faith, and perplexity accosted our educated minds. We wanted certitude, and would have been more comfortable with blueprints that assured success.

I prayed while driving, asking God to teach us something from this experience—anything at all—even if we never made contact with the pipe's keeper. We sought a man named Stanley Looking Horse who had entrusted his son Arvol (a man in his twenties) with the sacred object. If we found either person, I prayed that we could (if nothing else) have a good conversation about religious matters. My reflections were interrupted by Lame Foot's shouting "Ha Ho" as we neared the reservation. He pointed skyward to an eagle soaring above—its wide wings

seeming to wave us on. Our guide's exclamation was an
Indian equivalent to "Amen," or "Let it be so." He smiled
confidently and said: "We will meet with success."

Preparing for a Vision

We went immediately to Green Grass—hopeful of establishing contact with Stanley and arranging our sched-
ule for that night. The community itself was tucked away
in an area of small hills some distance from the main
highway and accessible only by means of a winding, dirt
road. A small shack would be on one hill, a trailer on another—a loghouse in the distance, a wooden one apart
from it. All were neatly kept—a Congregational church
overlooking the silent landscape.

Lame Foot directed us to a home whose occupants he
knew to be distant relatives. Drawing near he leaned out
the window and greeted one of the people. Conversing in
Lakota (the Sioux language), he learned that Stanley was
to be found elsewhere—at a trailer house beyond the next
rise. We set out in that direction, but found no one home.
Because it was late in the day, Lame Foot suggested we
first get accommodations for the night and then return to
Stanley's home later on. We did so, and came back to the
trailer at 7:30.

A fifty-year-old man with short-cropped hair, wearing a railroad cap, blue jeans and western shirt, greeted
us at the trailer. Lame Foot explained who we were and
that we had traveled far to pray with the pipe—Stanley
listening until our guide had finished his address. English interrupted what was until then an all-Indian dialogue when Stanley shook our hands and said: "Hello.
You can prepare for the sweatlodge by first picking sage"
(a fragrant, plentiful herb which grows wild and is used

in many Native religious ceremonies). Stanley informed us that he was co-caretaker of the pipe with his son Arvol (who was technically its nineteenth "caretaker"). He then parted and took the box of food we had brought—the usual offering given to religious practitioners.

After gathering several bundles of sage, we were directed to a house about a quarter of a mile west of Stanley's trailer. There he said we would undergo the sweatlodge ceremony—one of the seven sacred rites. He instructed Lame Foot to prepare the fire while he, Stanley, would attempt to find Arvol.

Driving toward the house at which Stanley pointed, we noticed several young people busy at play and little concerned about our presence on their land. My suspicion was that they had seen visitors around the dome-shaped sweatlodge on other occasions. We asked a young man where we might find wood to burn, and he led us to where we could help ourselves. He asked no questions.

Having gathered enough rocks and wood necessary for our purposes, Lame Foot directed my preparation of the fire—all of which, he said, was to be done with formulaic precision. The pit was dug directly in front of the sweatlodge door—an old buffalo skull with a broken horn staring coldly at the entrance.

I was told first to put a big rock on the west side of the pit, then to the north, east, and finally south. With those as a foundation, Lame Foot directed me to place a rock in the northwest corner, then the northeast, and so on. This back-and-forth pattern continued until we had erected something of a small, crude, pyramid of rocks. Lame Foot finished the preparations by stacking the collected wood around the pyramid—again beginning in the west and proceeding until a conical-shaped tepee was formed. He started the fire while praying (in Lakota) for his family back home and for blessings upon what we were to undertake.

The fire was glowing about 9 P.M., the sun having set in one direction and the moon giving its full light in the other. Mosquitoes feasted on the three of us as we awaited Stanley's arrival in the chilly night air. Around 10 P.M., Stanley drove up alone and deposited his medicine "suitcase" outside a red metal shed which stood near the sweatlodge. In olden days, men's sacred possessions were carried in what was called a "medicine bundle"—a container made of animal hides sewn with sinew. His updated terminology was appropriate since what he brought was, in fact, an old brown leather suitcase.

Lame Foot asked Stanley for a drink of water and motioned me to accompany the co-caretaker. We entered the home and Stanley looked around the kitchen—moving pots and pans and sundry other objects lying about the room. Silence was broken when Stanley stopped, looked at me and said (as if to read my mind): "Can't find a clean glass!" Locating a dirty one, he rinsed it out and handed it to me: "Take a drink of water if you want." He filled a bucket and I took Lame Foot the drink he requested. Meanwhile, Stanley drove away.

We waited a half-hour for his return and fought off swarms of mosquitoes as we moved to keep warm. Finally, the co-caretaker arrived and poured us hot black coffee which he carried in a pot. We sat there drinking the brew for about thirty minutes until Stanley said: "I guess Arvol isn't going to come. We might as well begin." (If Arvol knew we were there, or if he was otherwise occupied, we never learned. Younger Indian people sometimes camp within the popular ideology of rejecting things Christian, so Arvol's absence might have been on these grounds.)

Out of the suitcase he drew a twist of sweetgrass, lit it, and incensed the fire, the sweatlodge, the red shed, the medicine suitcase, and each of us. All the while, he prayed aloud. Extinguishing the incense, Stanley proceeded to undress—retaining only his undershorts. We were told to do likewise. Lame Foot, however, declined participating in the ceremony, as he stated that the pipe was too holy and that he was too much of a sinner. He had many evil thoughts infecting his mind and did not hold a firm purpose of amendment (so he said). Because of this, he did not wish to expose himself to the pipe's wrath. Retribution would be exacted upon those who did not reverence the pipe and obey good ways. Consequently, Lame Foot stayed outside the lodge and served in the helpful capacity of answering requests made by Stanley from within.

We placed a sprig of sage on our right ear (a custom which favorably identifies people to "spirits") and entered the lodge in a clockwise direction. I was told to sit on the western side which was facing the door (the door being directly in the path of the fire on the east). My colleague sat on the south side, while Stanley assumed his position near the door on the east. Upon entering we uttered (one after another) the prayerful phrase *mitak' oyassin* ("all are relatives")—a statement likewise common to many other religious ceremonies. As I crouched to get inside, Lame Foot held my arm and said: "Chew on sage; it will prevent you from collapsing." His advice was more than appreciated during the ritual which ensued.

Prayer and Purification

Once inside the lodge, our bodies shifted for a position affording the most comfort which, owing to the cramped space, was minimal. We had earlier spread sage upon the dirt floor and whisked away the variety of insects which angrily greeted our intrusion. Thus, we sat around the pit within the lodge awaiting Lame Foot's bringing of the heated rocks. My colleague was handed a pipe which Stanley had drawn from the suitcase, and was told to touch each rock passed through the door with the pipe stem. Upon touching each rock, my friend was instructed to say "All are relatives"—to which, we assented with "Hau" ("Yes," "Indeed," etc.). In fact, whenever anyone or anything would pass in or out of the lodge, these words were uttered.

Lame Foot used a pitchfork to carry the red, glowing rocks and Stanley pulled them across the floor and into the pit by means of deer antlers. When all the rocks had been placed in the center of the pit, Lame Foot closed the door and we were in total darkness. Stanley began the inside ritual by scattering cedar chips onto the hot coals, and this produced a pleasing (if smoky) aroma within the chamber. Lame Foot was told to open the flap, and our choking was prevented by a gust of wind which chased away the dense fumes. After a few moments the flap was closed and Stanley then proceeded to take a dipper from the nearby bucket of water and sprinkle the rocks.[7]

My experience of sauna baths paled in comparison to the steam which filled our small enclosure. Breathing through the nose I found impossible as the hot air seemed to be ablaze. Lame Foot's suggesting I chew sage proved to be my salvation, as the twigs (and saliva they produced) were natural filters for the intense heat which engulfed us.

7. Some groups combine herbs with the water and consider inhalation as additionally medicinal.

The traditional ceremony of purification continued to be a powerful test of physical endurance. People have, in fact, been forced to leave the sweatlodge due to exhaustion while others have completely passed out during the experience. I prayed for the power to remain.

After generously sprinkling the rocks, Stanley prayed at great length in his native tongue—afterward asking my colleague to make a prayer. When this was finished, the co-caretaker sprinkled more water on the stones and we were once again jarred with furnace-like vapors. Lame Foot was asked to open the flap—the evening's cool air providing us with welcome, refreshing, but temporary relief. Stanley offered us a drink which I gladly rinsed with—having chewed a sprig of sage watered by some animal of the plains. (Selectivity in reaching for sage was impossible due to the darkness.)

Our break completed, Stanley asked for the flap to be closed. Darkness once again prevailed, and steam once again struggled to overcome us. After praying himself, Stanley requested that I now make a prayer.

The lodge's red hot "altar" is said to represent the power of *Wakan Tanka,* as, indeed, the four elements of air, earth, fire, and water combine to produce an intense feeling of naked energy. Aliveness was inescapably felt as throbbing flesh pounded the fact of existence, and fragrant sage suggested its divine authorship.

In attempting to express my innermost spirit, I realized why Lame Foot was reluctant to participate. Asphyxiation was difficult enough to prevent while just sitting there. Drawing breath to speak was an even more painful challenge. I now knew why many a participant had failed the test of purification and had fled the lodge in physical and spiritual pain. I was pleased, then, to find the power to say: "Grandfather, Great Spirit, Father of Jesus, we

send our pitiful voices to you asking for help in our lives
... help to learn your will ... and help to do it ... in the
service of your people. Look upon your creatures—the
four-leggeds of the earth, and the two-leggeds—and bless
all who turn to you for power. Help us walk the good, red
road, the path of Jesus." Water on the stones followed my
prayer, and Stanley again voiced his own spiritual sentiments prior to asking for the flap to be opened.

Lame Foot was told to light the pipe and he did so
with an ember from the fire outside the lodge. Stanley received the lit pipe and handed it to my colleague who in
turn handed it to me. Both of us took several puffs, and
Stanley finished what was left of the tobacco—emptying
the ashes into the pit. Lame Foot was handed the pipe,
and Stanley said there was still water in the bucket which
had to be used. And so, the flap was closed and steam was
summoned from the rocks.

This was the fourth and final sequence of confinement, purgation, prayer, and release. The flap was
opened, and Stanley exited, saying "All are relatives" as
he passed through the entrance. My friend and I did ex-
actly the same—leaving the lodge counter-clockwise. As
we dressed (having inadequately dried our perspiration-
soaked bodies with sage), Lame Foot approached me and
said: "As I stood outside the door, I listened to your prayer.
And when you prayed, the entire sky lit up. It was quite a
sight to see." Being inside the lodge at the time, we could
hardly contradict his statement.

Waiting for a Vision

It was midnight by the time we were dressed, and the
day's heat had long since vanished. We felt as though we
had just gone swimming, left the water, and clothed our-

selves without first drying. (I reminded myself to bring a towel the next time I undertook the sweatlodge ceremony.) The clear, cold, night air struck a persistent, penetrating chill. After several minutes of silence, Stanley and Lame Foot very casually exchanged information about family matters. When their conversation stopped, Stanley said: "Now I'll go get the key and let you see the pipe."

He headed for the house which had earlier supplied us with water, and returned carrying a powerful flashlight. Approaching the red shed, the co-caretaker unlocked the door. The dirt floor only allowed a partial opening as Stanley squeezed himself inside and set the flashlight on an overhead rack. We heard him moving around until shortly he appeared at the door, came out, and motioned to my colleague. I sat with Stanley and Lame Foot while my friend was in the shed.

No urgency or hurriedness or uneasiness was evident during this entire period. Stanley and Lame Foot continued talking leisurely about different events while I respectfully listened. In the meantime, I wondered what awaited me within the shed. Relatively few Indian people were allowed this experience, and even fewer non-Indians. My ordination to the diaconate was a week away, and there I sat—prepared to be in the presence of the Sacred Lady's gift from heaven.

I remembered hearing from some people that the pipe was alive, and that in approaching it the most strict reverence must be given lest punishment be meted out. Years earlier, Black Elk's wife had even warned her daughter not to cross the path of the pipe's caretaker—for one could not be sure if their hidden darknesses of spirit would be known and scourged by the angrily purifying sacred object. The sweatlodge ceremony and pipe smoking (with some variation) were fairly common to Indian religious practice throughout North America. But actual nearness to the original pipe was no ordinary happening. While reflecting on these and other aspects of the pipe tradition, my friend emerged from the shed and was told to say "All are relatives." He was then directed to circle the enclosure—exiting east, moving south, then west, and finally around to the north. When he joined us, I was motioned to enter.

The Sacred Pipe

I slowly squeezed through the door and stood under the flashlight's full beam. Old auto parts and other yard-cluttering materials were piled inside with no particular order (apparent to me, that is). The light was aimed at a tripod made of pine which stood perhaps three to four feet high and which held a kettle-shaped buffalo hide. A flap covered the kettle's wide circumference. Lifting the flap, I found the container empty—wondering, all of a sudden, if the contents of this Indian tabernacle, this Holy of Holies, had eluded me or disappeared. I closed the flap and stood upright.

I then noticed, off to the side, a large bundle of what seemed to be fish-netting piled on a bench. I realized that this was the medicine bundle removed from the buffalo container. It was not a fish net, but that was its appearance—red ribbons tied throughout the white webbing. Deep within the bundle was the pipe itself—other sacred objects wrapped, companion-like, over the generations as special gifts to God and the people. I stood in quiet prayer gazing at what lay before me.

For years I had studied about this sacred religious tradition, discussed it with scholars, and participated with Indian people in pipe ceremonies. Christianity was the only other spirituality with which I was intimately involved. I felt to be in somewhat of an Indian Holy Land or North American mosque. Here was Jerusalem and Calvary—but in a different place, with a different appearance.

I stood on the dirt floor of a rundown shed, far from the twentieth century, viewing sacred simplicity. Here was the symbol of faith for Sioux Indians beyond memory—as rich in spiritual meaning as any Native religious tradition of North America. Nothing glimmered. Nothing moved. Nothing spoke but the centuries-told tale of God's promised presence.

The vision of faith, it is said, can proclaim the handiwork of God within creation. There in the shed, a voice of faith could cry gratitude for having a tangible sign from a God who listens. Dirt, stones, wood, and cloth in orderly disarray seemed to reflect the frailty so needful of divine support. Bethlehem suddenly seemed so close.

I carried an eagle feather with me and made with it a sign of the cross over the medicine bundle—a spontaneous gesture and reverencing moment toward the two religious traditions which so forcefully spoke to me at the time. Asking for help to nourish its lived-reality, I exited the shed praying "All are relatives" and circled my way back to Lame Foot, Stanley, and my brother Jesuit.

Upon my arrival back to the group, Stanley entered the shed and replaced the medicine bundle within the buffalo hide. Scraping the door shut, he fastened the padlock and went up to the house. Gone but a few minutes, he returned with four cups and more hot black coffee. I thanked Stanley for allowing us to pray with him and asked how he became the pipe's caretaker. He willingly told us of his conversion.

The Pipe's Caretaker

One day several years ago, an ailing relative by the name of Elk Head came to Stanley and asked to be cured. No money was available to pay for a doctor. Stanley's mother (Lucy Bad Warrior) had received the pipe from her own mother (Martha) and used to help people with her special medicines. Elk Head thought that Stanley had preserved this knowledge and could therefore be of some assistance, but Stanley had wasted much of his life on alcohol.

Feeling helpless and ashamed, Stanley went into the hills in search of herbs his mother used for Elk Head's sickness. He looked all over but could not find what he wanted. Finally, he sat down and saw some eagles flying in the distance. He got up and went home to pray with his mother's pipe that he would find the herbs he sought. Stanley then drove his car in the general vicinity of the flying eagles, stopped, and got out of the car. There at his feet grew the desired plant. He was able to cure Elk Head. Since that time, he has properly administered the pipe following the tradition of eighteen previous caretakers.

No one is allowed to view the sacred bundle without first undergoing the purification of the sweatlodge—conducted by either Stanley or his son. In fact, most Native religious traditions share this cleansing rite. It frequently preceded any important undertaking. Entrance to the padlocked shed is carefully guarded—even though legends associated with its transgression serve as warning enough for people to stay away.

This responsibility is, then, an awesome one. As unwilling heir of the sacred pipe, Stanley had fled the demands he knew it would make. Unable to help a relative as a result (a felt tragedy among the Sioux since kinship ties are so strong), the keeper was poignantly confronted with the lifeless poverty of alcohol. But Stanley remembered that his legacy was originally given by God to "make the people live"—and turning to it in desperation, he found rebirth. He no longer drinks liquor.

Stanley said he was honored that two Catholic religious participated in the pipe ceremony, that we were the only ones to ever be in its presence, and that we have always prayed to the same God—just in different ways. Stanley insisted that our two spiritual traditions were harmonious with each other but that the evil spirit tries to bring division. (This might have been Stanley's way of condemning those who claim Christianity to be irreconcilable with the older Siouan tradition. Lame Foot added that Stanley belonged to the Congregational church we passed earlier in the day.)

Before parting, we were invited to the Sun Dance (a sacred rite) scheduled for the next month—an invitation we were honored to receive. It was to be a private celebration rather than the commercialized ceremony prevalent around the country. At about two in the morning we shook hands good-bye.

On the road to Pine Ridge eight hours later, Lame Foot pointed overhead and smilingly shouted: "*Hoka hey!* (Let's go!) We'll have a safe trip home." An eagle was flying directly above us.

PART TWO

Seeking a New Consciousness

*Don Juan laughed scornfully before answering.
It seemed that he was trying hard to be patient
with me. "Maiz-pinto, crystals, and feathers are
mere toys in comparison with an ally," he said.
"These power objects are necessary only when a
man does not have an ally. It is a wise time to
pursue them especially for you. You should be
trying to get an ally; when you succeed, you will
understand what I am telling you now. Power objects are like a game for children."*

*"Don't get me wrong, Don Juan," I protested.
"I want to have an ally, but I also want to know
everything I can. You yourself said that knowledge is power."*

*"No!" he said emphatically. "Power rests on
the kind of knowledge one holds. What is the
sense of knowing things that are useless?"*

The Teachings of Don Juan

The Teachings of Don Juan by Carlos Castaneda was
a book instantly and enthusiastically received by spiri-
tually-hungry youth of the late 1960's and early 1970's. Although the work's accuracy was questioned, it still

seemed to address the plight of many people. Carole King's "You've Got a Friend" was released at the same time and sounded like an appropriate answer-song to Castaneda's call for companionship. Moviegoers of this period likewise saw Don Juan's wisdom reinforced when films depicted contemporary life as empty. Castaneda's characters promised an alternative way to be-in-the-world.

An example from one such film shows a woman tearfully leaving her man. He had neatly explained why marriage should not, as yet, be a serious consideration for them. Realizing the hopelessness of trying to set up life with him, the woman agonizingly said in parting: "If you're so damn smart, why can't you make me happy?" Her reproof was based on more than just the marriage question. It was related to an interpersonal dimension which the man, for all his brilliance, simply lacked.

This helter-skelter, Vietnam War period was a time of social disorientation that has still not entirely run its course. Lives had enjoyed a fair amount of material well-being. This, combined with "getting an education," formed a presumption within many that some type of "togetherness" or community or "happiness" would naturally result. Since such interpersonal union did not always develop, disillusionment followed. War escalated along with assassins, and Woodstock's four-letter assessment of society received symbolic support—experimental lifestyles proliferating as frequently as the daily raids on Hanoi.

Bright, inquisitive minds had begun to perceive traditional securities as highly questionable and transient. Something more certain or stable or truly enduring was sought anew (or else considered impossible to find). And Castaneda's work (six books in all) rode the current of these times. He championed a return to the "natural state" which seemed to be preserved by Indian people. His writing suggested that mind/life expansion was attainable through, among other things, a carefully-religious use of drugs.

Alcohol seemed more befitting the bourgeois generations which had been found wanting, so marijuana was loftily raised (almost as a sign) in outward defiance. Hierarchically, LSD reigned as a type of modern sacrament *par excellence*—promising a fullness of vision which was denied the uninitiated. Other drugs became widely used and, when not injurious to life, allured many into thinking that a significantly new consciousness had been discovered. Though many critical judgments can be levied against this period of drug use, there can be no doubt that much of the trial-and-error process was symptomatic of a deeper, call it "religious," quest.

With this admittedly brief historical background, it should still be clear why Indian America cast considerable appeal. Resistant to pressures of conformity, and regarded as the epitome of counter-culture, Native peoples were also vaguely known to have mastered some control over drugs. Castaneda brought this dimly-lit world onto bookshelves across America, as a vast audience accepted his proposition that a new, liberating spirituality was within reach.

Peyote Spirituality

Even though the several books which arose from *The Teachings of Don Juan* were novel introductions for most Americans to the use of drugs for religious purposes, the spiritual tradition at their core was already centuries-old among different tribes. Alcoholic beverages, though used for secular purposes, were ceremonially employed by southwestern and Mexican tribes. So, too, jimsonweed was known among an assortment of groups from California to Meso-America—its effects sought for either pleasure or more serious concerns (e.g., predicting the future, curing the sick, communicating with supernatural powers). Other narcotic mushrooms, beans, leaves, and plants were part of this complex of Native religious pharmacology, but none of these attained the popularity of peyote.

Variously pronounced "pea'-oat" or "pay-oat'-ee," this carrot-shaped root is native to the deserts of central and northern Mexico (extending even into Texas). Its tip rises above the ground and is called a mescal or peyote "button." Either this tip or the whole plant may be consumed. It can, moreover, be prepared as a spinach-like porridge, or brewed into a sort of greenish tea. Its mescaline content is valued for producing what non-peyotists call "hallucinogenic effects." Peyote eating is thought by some to be the fastest growing and largest Indian religious movement today (adherents are said to number over 200,000). Others, however, point to its decline.

Sometimes simply referred to as "peyotism" or the peyote "cult," the tradition legally organized itself after the turn of this century into what is now called the Native American Church. A survey of North America would reveal its presence throughout the American and Canadian plains, the southeast, the Great Lakes region, and a small section of the east coast. Migration to cities outside these areas has also extended peyote influence beyond the reservation milieu (which originally gave it birth).

The Kiowa and Comanche of Oklahoma are credited with giving impetus to peyote in the United States (around 1870), and from them the cult spread rather quickly. When Black Elk of the Sioux worked as a Christian missionary some forty years later, he found "peyote people" already established among his own tribe. In fact, the cult's golden age of ascendancy appears to have occurred at this time. A complex set of social and spiritual conditions seems to have made the Native American Church a healing of Indian wounds that had festered too long.

The Indian world of the late 1800's was a recently defeated one. Confinement to reservations was overseen and enforced by military conquerors. Stress on acculturation was stimulated by educational institutions, church groups, and government agencies—all de-emphasizing anything perceived as traditional. Many religious ceremonies were, if not outlawed, forcibly discouraged. In short, an entire way of life was being accosted from all sides—a way of life that tribes were unwilling to forfeit. Traditionally the lifeblood of a people's identity, religious ritual would remain as a last compromise—other cultural traits being more negotiable.

Origin stories which relate the coming of peyote vary—but all point to a belief now cherished and clung to by its users—namely that the Supernatural took pity on the Indian and so decided to communicate spiritual power to the people through this special plant. Newly subjugated tribes could especially appreciate so important a gift. Hence, the simultaneous appearance of the peyote and Christian traditions (both regarded as a light in the darkness of social decay) seemed a providential outreach to tribes feeling supernaturally abandoned.

As mentioned earlier, there appears to be little evidence showing Indian rejection of the Christian myth. The proposition that God took flesh in Jesus and taught people how to live seemed quite possible and could indeed be considered "good news." On a fairly universal basis, in fact, Indian people saw particular merit in such a story. Most tribes conceived the Supernatural to be multi-faceted, so the story of Jesus was often accepted as a very important revelation. It was certainly possible, they thought, and even very needed! Its formulation in specifically Native terms however remained to be done.

The externals of Christian practice (be they of Protestant denominations or Catholic) were largely European-based. Indian people adapted to foreign modes, but some harbored a spiritual restlessness that yearned for Native expression. When word of the "Peyote Way" was brought by visitors, a certain hope was kindled that herein might be the awaited revelation, the binding of Native and Christian ways. Whether the cult did represent this union, or whether needy individuals strove to make it so, Peyote missionaries met with considerable success in spreading what some followers call an Indian version of Christianity.[1]

All this is a broad survey of peyotism's emergence and spread. Three points are worth summarizing: (1) the cult has its roots in Mexico and the southwest, (2) it spread quite rapidly at the turn of this century, and (3) it was adapted from tribe to tribe with a strongly Christian flavor. This last aspect needs to be clarified, since followers of the peyote way express their practice with some variation.

---

1. John Slocum's "Shaker religion," founded in the 1880's around Puget Sound, is considered by its members to truly represent Indian Christianity. With roots in traditional northwest coast religious practices, the group resembles Christian Pentecostalism's emphasis on being "slain in the Spirit." Indian Shakers will fall onto the floor quivering, trance-like, and sing. Healings, likewise, figure prominently within this practice.

Peyote Membership

Just as Christianity has witnessed different render-
ings among diverse groups of people, so Peyote has
achieved unique adaptation within different tribal contexts. For example, attendance at a meeting among the
Osage, though similar in some ways, will not be duplicat-
ed among the Arapaho. Whereas, for instance, the Catholic Mass will follow the same procedures in both New
York and Chicago, Peyote meetings will reveal more nu-
ance. Consequently, a comment is in order which will indicate these shared and dissimilar features.

Peyote gatherings might be held anywhere—someone's home, a tepee, a church owned by the group, or any
place considered safe from interruption. Typically, however, a large, conical-shaped tepee is preferred, as it sym-
bolizes traditional Indian life (at least of the Plains area).
It provides, in addition, a control over the number of people able to participate. Thus, gatherings are generally
small (and open to non-Indian guests who are invited).

A key distinction within Peyote practice among the
Sioux is the bipartite division of adherents into groups
called the "Half Moon" and the "Cross Fire" (so named
because of designs on their respective altars). These designations might broadly be analogous to "high" and "low"
church Anglicans. Other tribes show comparable differences. People from one group can attend meetings of the
other, but prefer a particular orientation. Spelling out
some basic contrasts between the two groups should illustrate why the above analogy seems more or less appropriate.

The Half Moon "fireplace" (as a division is called)
has, over the years, tended to retain a religious emphasis

more in keeping with their tribe's earlier spiritual tradition. Rather than refer to the leader as a "minister" (as Cross Fire people often do), this fireplace is presided over by someone respectfully called a "road man." No sign of membership, other than presence at ceremonies, is insisted upon. Likewise, meetings are conducted in which much singing, little talking, and few interruptions occur. The road man orchestrates the eating of peyote and the general flow of the gathering (if practical, in the Native language). The pipe tradition (and other elements of the earlier belief system) is reconciled with certain fundamentalist themes of Christianity which characterize the group's creed.

Cross Fire people, by contrast, are organized more along the lines of an institutional model. Baptism of its members, a strict moral code, and ordination of its ministers are part of the elaborately written canons which maintain the group's tradition. A Bible is within clear view of participants as it remains on the altar throughout the ceremony. The "minister" exhorts members during the session with sermonettes based on a fairly literal interpretation of Scripture. Gospel songs might also be sung (in English) and interruptions (leaving the tepee for various purposes) are far more frequent than among the Half Moon. The breakfast which always follows peyote meetings also admits greater variety, as coffee, crackers, cookies, or candy would be served along with the traditional beef, corn, fruit, and water.

Other differences could be noted, fine distinctions made, and comparative studies drawn up. A volume could even be written for the peculiarities of each peyote group that gathers. Literature is already available which does, in fact, present such studies. But the purpose of these reflections is to make an excursion into religious experience itself and attempt to tap the lifeblood of an Indian spirituality which still remains vital—despite modern trends that challenge the need for anything but material comfort.

The section which follows is intended to recreate, through means of the written word, a sense of participation within the peyote lodge. With many people claiming to have met God in such a place, vision-seekers would do well to at least make a visit.

In the Peyote Lodge

Having been invited to a peyote meeting conducted by Half Moon practitioners, I willingly accepted. Various reasons prompted my ready reply—friendship, curiosity, and religious interest (to name a few). Foremost, however, was a gnawing dissatisfaction with debate over the propriety of Christian participation in a cult which some had actually labeled demonic. Knowing the sponsors of the affair to be good and friendly people, and knowing that they attributed much of their life-vision to the use of peyote, I felt obliged to be present.

A friend was going to make a long journey, and the purpose of gathering for the peyote ritual was to pray for his safe return. A large tepee was to be the setting for our ceremony—pitched next to an abandoned schoolhouse in an out-of-the-way spot on the Pine Ridge Reservation. Situated a half-mile from the main highway, the peyote lodge was hidden out of sight from the several houses which dotted the hills beyond.

Arriving about an hour before the ritual was to begin, we found the sponsoring family eagerly making sure that all was in order. The ceremony would last all night, and so firewood needed to be in good supply. The schoolhouse would serve as a kitchen in which the peyote would be readied and the breakfast prepared. So it, too, needed organization. Participants from other reservations were arriving, and they had to be properly welcomed. All in all, this organizational period heightened anticipation. The placement of materials in order, muffler-less cars chugging to a halt, quiet greetings, and hushed conversations (all quite normal under other circumstances) appeared now as a many-splendored drama against the backdrop of the tepee.

We were asked to enter the lodge's warmth at 8 P.M., the sun having dropped along with the temperature just shortly before. The group who gathered was comprised mostly of people in their forties, although one infant, two teenagers, and several older persons were also in attendance. In all, thirty-five of us were propped against the tepee's circular wall—our faces aglow from the well-kindled fire which burned brightly in the center.

We were immediately informed by the road man (named Eagle Bear) as to how leadership was to be exercised. Directly across from the road man was the "fire man." His duty would be to guard the door from unwanted intruders. He was, moreover, responsible for keeping the fire alive.

Whenever a ceremonial object was to be used, cedar would be sprinkled on the fire. The person assigned to this task was known as the "cedar man," and he was positioned immediately to the left of Eagle Bear. A water drum (hide stretched over a half-filled iron kettle) was given to the "drummer"—seated to the right of the road man. I was third from Eagle Bear, separated by my friend in whose honor the meeting was held, and the cedar man.

Having welcomed everyone to the special event, Eagle Bear expressed kind thanks that God had given him sixty years of life and allowed him to preside over so sacred a gathering. "Long ago," we were told, "God gave Indian people the sacred medicine of peyote. We should eat the sacred medicine, as God wanted us to do."

My friend asked if he could bring along his sacred pipe for the ceremony—permission granted by the road man but needful of explanation for others who gathered. So Eagle Bear addressed the group:

> This pipe for the Sioux is very sacred. They don't call it the "peace pipe" at all. It is a "sacred pipe." I was taught by my grandfather not to call it the peace pipe because peace still doesn't prevail in this globe at all. But we will use it for the sacredness of it.

> We Sioux call it the sacred pipe. That's the proper word for it. As you recall, when Christ was born, they sang in heaven: "Peace on earth, good will to men." But King Herod killed a lot of children over him. Instead of having peace, that happens. Since that time, they have been having conflict. Peace is a very elusive word.

> We want to be saved—each one of us. Forgive us for our sins. Sometimes we will not accept Jesus in our hearts. We want to live in a good way in our homes, with our children—earning everything we need. Tonight, all these sacred things are coming to take place here.

A young couple had strong misgivings about the presence of the pipe in a peyote ritual, as it symbolized olden practices they thought should be better left alone. They threatened to depart and never return to this fireplace, but Eagle Bear and others assured them that all was proper in the eyes of God. I was reminded of conflicts within Christian churches about "updating" as these proceedings moved along. The road man's "pastoral touch" was impressive.

Since four different tribes were represented at this gathering, I knew only a couple of people. Most were, in fact, barely acquainted with one another. I made this reflection on the group's makeup after the pipe discussion had subsided. The warm fire created chamber-sounds of cracking, snapping, coal-red embers. Shadows danced against the tepee walls as eyes moved about the group asking silent questions.

From across the lodge, Eagle Bear was asked to dismiss from the gathering a middle-aged couple accused of being intoxicated. The man's request was seconded. Eagle Bear turned to the couple in question and suggested that they respond to the charges. Moved to tears, the husband said that they had been drinking but were not out of control. They had looked forward to this meeting and were ashamed of themselves for raising controversy and violating the ritual. Noticeably shaken, he pleaded that they be allowed to remain—pledging repentance and prayer. Eagle Bear listened until the man had entirely finished his appeal.

Waiting some time before speaking, the road man addressed the group and reflected on the sacredness of the ceremony and the necessity of having a proper disposition. Silence ensued, interrupted only by the fire man attending to his duties. The hour-long drama concluded with Eagle Bear's decision to let the couple stay—sensing the sincerity of their tears, apology, and strength to last the night. Hours later, the husband would (under the influence of peyote) pray aloud his regret for this incident. In addition a visibly intense prayer of thanksgiving would accompany his apology.

All of these events lasted a fairly long time. And so, unaccustomed to sitting on the ground for lengthy periods, I found myself shifting regularly to positions that would afford at lease some comfort. Stretching legs was not possible since many of us were directly behind the Half Moon altar—a half-circled, small mound of carefully etched dirt—at the outer center of which Eagle Bear presided.

The Night-Long Ceremony

It was about 10 P.M. when the road man started to sing—accompanied by drum-beating and the shaking of a gourd rattle. Since singing and percussion are believed to carry prayer to God, this communication would occur throughout the proceedings. Quiet meditation, though crucial, was not permitted to fall asleep.

The songs were all in Lakota and, as with many tribes, tended to be repetitious. One of them (translated) might just be a single thought like the following:

Savior Jesus is the only Savior.

Mantra-like, such verses seemed to focus praying minds. With eyes closed, people listened to high vibrato sounds which stung home important reflections:

God said in the beginning,
"Let there be light."
He meant it for you.

Traditional Christian prayer might shine forth at some point as members hear them feelingly cried and purposefully uttered.

After finishing his prayer-song, Eagle Bear distributed cigarette wrappers and tobacco, as ceremonial smoking was always part of the preliminary ritual. The man seated next to me offered to "roll" my smoke, but I declined, saying I thought I could manage. After dropping most of the tobacco, and nearly shredding the wrapper, I turned to my neighbor whose hand was already outstretched. Salvaging what he could, my ally presented me with a miniature perfect cigarette. Eagle Bear instructed us to light our smokes with embers from the fire and dispose of the butts by returning them to the cedar man (who, in turn, placed them in the fire). Having fewest puffs, I finished first—the rest of the group smoking in silence and listening to the road man's grandfatherly advice and smiling words of encouragement.

I wondered if our smoking was rooted in the more ancient pipe tradition which this fireplace had abandoned. Why would the practice be retained, but the ritual instrument be changed? Perhaps this act was a telling example of the compromise struck long ago. The old had given way to the new, but the wisdom associated with tradition had been preserved.

Interestingly, those who protested the pipe readily accepted tobacco and wrapper. Some appeared to know that their actions were invested with age-old solemnity. Others simply followed instructions and revealed little awareness of these considerations. I likened the scene to other churches, chapels, and assorted assemblies of people who were culturally far removed from this compatible gathering of peyote folk. Some seem ever so conscious of why certain practices and actions occur, and others seem to participate—out of habit? out of a sense of duty? for private reasons? because there's nothing else to do?

After another song, Eagle Bear motioned the fire man to let enter a woman who had prepared the sacred medicine. She presented him with a large, glass, chalice-like container with a spoon handle protruding from the top. The road man expressed much gratitude to her and the kitchen crew and stated how important their role was for the ceremony. After singing and praying, Eagle Bear took several spoonfuls of peyote and handed the container to the cedar man. Singing (always in Lakota) and drumming continued while the peyote was passed around clockwise.

I especially noticed the cedar man's eating of the sacred medicine. With each spoonful and swallow (he took four), his face became contorted and his expression greatly pained. I made certain not to eat that day because I understood that peyote frequently caused vomiting (members having receptacles in case such "air bags" were needed). The cedar man's anguished look gave the appearance of something lodged in his throat. He seemed to be welling up all his energy simply to swallow. Within moments, however, the chalice was extended my way.

Looking into the mixture, I was reminded of what might be imagined as milky-spinach. Prayerfully hoping that my physical reaction would respect the tradition and not embarrass me, I followed suit by taking four spoonfuls—one right after another. As anticipated, the initial, pungent taste of peyote immediately summoned my system to vomit—my fasting for the day proving to be a timely decision. Without exhibiting any noticeable reaction, I finished my portion without incident. Once swallowed, though, nausea did not persist. Having the medicine for less than two minutes, I returned the spoon into the chalice and passed it on.

Each participant seemed to take about the same amount and then pass the chalice onward. Different individuals were given the water drum, and kept somewhat of a pulsating song-prayer alive. The fire man was handed the empty container and he exited. All the while—drum-dum-dum-dum! drum-dum-dum-dum! drum-dum-dum-dum!—sometimes fast, sometimes not. The tepee flap was closed, and none of the singing-beats could escape. We breathed percussion, as high-pitched songs joined base drum-sounds. I forgot to think about the time.

Later on, a teapot was presented at the tepee flap, allowed entry, and given to Eagle Bear. Because the medicine's bitter properties dry the mouth, a special peyote tea would partially slake our thirst. Perhaps because of dilution, perhaps because the taste was no longer foreign, the drink was soothing—a common cup passed along with the teapot from one person to the next.

The road man reflected aloud how fortunate we were to have such a drink, and added:

When the peyote starts working, this music that comes out of the singers will be good for the soul—good for what ails you—good for your problems.

As the fire man rakes the coals, I'm going outside to pray to the four directions. When I come back in, we are going to eat medicine again. It is the custom of this fireplace.

Taking leave of the group, the road man exited and returned within a very short time. After being seated, Eagle Bear asked the fire man to bring in more medicine. Once again, the same pattern was followed as earlier in the night—except that the fire man was noticeably absent.

Prior to when the chalice was passed, angry voices could be heard along with the sound of a car motor some distance outside the lodge. But they died down, and Eagle Bear commenced eating. A young mother dabbed her infant's tongue with the mixture—puckered cheeks stinging with a taste quite different from its earlier milk.

Drum-dum-dum-dum! Drum-dum-dum-dum! High voices. Whining-like words. Penetrating. Constant. Fire-flames. Embers gray-red. Faces with shut eyes. Warm stillness. Tepee-tallness. Good people. Religious praying. Stop! Silence—except for the sound of wood-eating fire.

The road man acknowledged the good job done by the drummers and singers who, he said, helped us realize how powerful the medicine was. After paying this compliment, Eagle Bear told us about the nature of the disturbance outside. Troublemakers had spotted the tepee and planned to disrupt the meeting. Physical violence erupted, but was kept in check by the fire man and male relatives of the sponsor. The road man spoke of how there is an ever-present struggle between good and evil. It was evil that was trying to stop our holy ceremony, but peyote would not permit it to overcome.

Since there seemed to be a pause in the proceedings, my friend asked if I wanted to get a breath of fresh air. I nodded and rose, realizing that I had for some time not been concerned with the earlier discomfort of sitting cross-legged on the ground. Opening the flap and leaving the lodge's warmth, we greeted the chilly moon which shone white above us.

Spending but a short time in the cool, clean, night air, I was surprised that no sense of fatigue accompanied me into the late hours. I knew it was getting on, but time seemed suspended within the tepee. What filled my consciousness was not the demands of ordinary duties, but rather the immediacy of lodge participation. Within the tepee, all that mattered was the experience of now—the distractions of daily life barred from intrusion. Contemplating these thoughts, I hastened to rejoin the praying group.

Singing was begun after the road man shared some insights on the topic of being a religious person. Different individuals tape-recorded his remarks as they had done with songs from throughout the night (a common practice so that one can replay a particularly good chant or talk long after a given meeting). The sacred medicine was distributed a last time, and the procedure remained the same.

Just a few days earlier, I had been in Chicago—nicknamed the "Windy City" long ago because of the boastful pride of its inhabitants. Situated on Lake Michigan, the city's majestic skyline seems to command a reverence from all approaches. Entering by air, land, or water, people are awed by the many buildings that suggest the heavens are securely attached to the earth. It occurred to me that modern genius had improved upon history and fulfilled the dream of Babel's once-thwarted architects.

A popular song had convincingly proposed that listeners accept Chicago as their "kind of town." The city could claim all the wonders of twentieth-century life. And yet its appeal seemed common to most every other metropolis. All just appear to be variations on a theme of busy people attending to their concerns within different-sized temples—monolithic structures with gazes that suggest durability or power. In such cities, meaning or security becomes associated with elaborate rituals related to secular sacraments. These might include the sacred profanity of winning subway sanction or corporate approval, acquitting oneself at tavern tribunals, knowing one's place within the hierarchy of economic enterprise, or simply surviving the liturgy of street existence.

Thoughts and images of this nature rushed through my mind as I stared at the lodge's fire. Here was uncompetitive belonging. Here was the feel of firm earth and warm togetherness. Here the sights and sounds, incentives and goals of urban America had no life—except as a memory twisting my mind and, like a bad dream, not going away.

According to textbooks, poverty's weakness defined Indian life. But as I surveyed the faces of lodge people, strength and richness would smile back. In a few days I would return to the material comforts of Chicago, aware of the wealth that this fireplace knew God extended.

By now, consuming peyote was not difficult—not easy, of course, but far less of a challenge. The drum-singing reminded me of the childhood experiment of having someone close his eyes, hold his nose, and state what he had been given to eat—an apple or onion; as with this experiment, so with the drum-singing. Visual, auditory, and olfactory stimulation seem so enveloping that the power of taste becomes greatly diminished.

Drum-dum-dum-dum. Drum-dum-dum-dum. Da-da-da-da. Da-da-da-da. Smoke wisps. Flap closed. Infant-sleep. Altar-neat. Crying throat. People-warmth. God sees. Here is. Burning moments. Shared. The road man signaled silence and gave what was to be a final exhortation.

> Jesus Christ, on the third day he arose, sits at the
> right hand of God to quicken the dead. All of us go
> through that, regardless. Jesus Christ made that
> road for us. Peyote teaches that this is the road.
> St. Peter in heaven, he watches that gate. I hope
> you learn that way through this worship. Every-
> body is going to be healthy and good. God is test-
> ing you.

Some singing followed this counsel, and I could hear bird
choruses from outside. Morning had awakened.

Thanksgiving

After a period of silence, different individuals would
address the gathering and express gratitude that God had
been so present. People acknowledged that Eagle Bear
had officiated well. The sacred medicine had once again
made members deeply appreciative that God communicated with the people and permitted such closeness. The
group all seemed to express a profound sense of well-being, as the relaxed atmosphere now permitted a more casual exchange. Eagle Bear even assumed a less-formal
posture and stretched out (as far as the limited space
would allow).

The flap was soon opened and, along with morning
light, let enter the sponsoring couple. They carried four
items: a bucket of water, a large bowl of cooked hamburger, and similar-sized containers of corn and berries. The
bucket of water held a ladle, while the bowls had a spoon
within each. All four gifts were presented to Eagle Bear,
and he thanked them, saying the kitchen-people had, as
expected, performed their task most successfully.

The road man ate from the bowls one by one—passing clockwise first the hamburger, then the corn, berries, and water. Each person was to take as much as was desired, this being a type of communal breakfast in the most literal sense. We all used the same three spoons and ladle. I was moved that Eagle Bear took time to address me at this time and say that I had conducted myself quite appropriately and did not seem out of place at all. When the last container was emptied, people began to leave. The ceremony was finished. At about 9 A.M., I left the tepee.

Others have reported that peyote people will frequently socialize after a meeting and that sunglasses will be worn by a good many. The same observation applied here. Since pupil dilation occurs with the eating of the plant, eyes are quite sensitive to whatever light may be present. With the sun brightly warming the earth, individuals leisurely wandered about or conversed in small groups. Some napped on car seats, while others smoked as they leaned against a tree or truck. The scene was one of tranquil community—grandfathers quietly reminiscing, younger men exchanging information about work (or lack of it), people introducing themselves for the first time, and women tending younger children while trying to prepare upcoming lunch.

Wandering from one huddled group to the next, I learned that several people were departing for another meeting to be held that night—some one hundred and fifty miles distant. Conversations revealed different understandings of peyote, as one said it was Jesus, another the Holy Spirit, or the food of angels, while some simply claimed that it was the way through which God speaks to people. All agreed that we were much indebted to the sacred medicine.

Eagle Bear's father had been an ardent Catholic, and

most of the group pointed to some past or sporadic tie with that tradition. Some had clashed with their local priest over some issue and turned to peyote where they felt more at home. Others still occasionally attended Mass. All were (whatever their previous affiliation) very clearly concerned about religious practice, the thought of having none seen as pitiable, unwhole, or not on a "life-road." Sociologically, the people of this fireplace were considered "full bloods" (i.e., either they had little trace-able intermarriage with non-Indians, or their social be-havior was not patterned on Euro-American models). Their congeniality made a forcefully positive impression on me as we gathered for a noon meal.

The sponsors had obviously expended much effort in organizing the occasion since a plentiful table awaited the group which by now had tripled in size. An abun-dance of chicken, salads, vegetables, frybread, cake and jello was pure torture for several wagging dogs. They ig-nored the swats, shouts, and pushes ceremonially direct-ed their way and, after a while, their persistence paid off. After all, there was enough to go around. This was a time of gladness and sharing for *all* present.

After thanking the sponsors, I departed around 2 P.M. Driving home, I felt that time had slipped by very quick-ly, and no sense of exhaustion was uppermost in mind. Rather, the reigning reflection seemed somehow fixed on the night's warm fire and praying people. Alone now, the closeness of others in an intensely common, religious en-terprise was growingly removed. Houses and highway sped by as I anticipated resuming life as before. The bond of the lodge was now an infant memory—with the pas-sage of time, an old recollection.

For some of the people, lifepaths often seemed a road of pain and suffering—with peyote serving as a soothing relief. For others, gathering overcame the paralysis of loneliness. The lodge of tears and joy revealed itself as a microcosm of human longing—the fire in our midst a burning symbol of heart-pourings heavenward.

Since the ritual consumption of peyote is so carefully handled and is not addictive, the Native American church has overcome legal questions that have arisen. As mentioned, it seemed to me that peyotists demonstrated very Christian behavior. In fact, "drug use" did not emerge as the reason why these people were so disposed. On the contrary, peyotists showed a praiseworthy disdain for illicit drug-taking.

From my point of view, this Native American church required a prayerful involvement that many non-Indians would probably find too rigorous. It was this involvement, and not the death-dealing illusions of drug-use, that impressed itself on me. Indeed, Christian peyotists would be offended by criticisms leveled at their peyote-consumption in much the same way that other Christians would feel hurt if it was said that they "got drunk" on consecrated wine.

As I returned from the experience, I wondered if a peyote ritual could occur without peyote even being used (although peyotists would probably consider such a thought as heresy). As it was, however, the exotic aspect of peyote-consumption did serve to punctuate a ceremony whose essence was actually already quite familiar to me. I had been with a community of human beings sincerely engaged in prayer and song to their Maker. I had participated in a kind of consummate, para-liturgical religious exercise.

While with the peyote people, I observed the expression of varied needs and an admission of dependence on something beyond even the world-lodge. I began to realize why different Christian denominations were newly appreciating the spiritual wisdom inherent to the sacred pipe and Native American church traditions. Instead of striving to convert Native practices into Western forms, Christian groups had become more sophisticated than in times past. They were now better able to discriminate between theological and cultural divergences.

I had spent the night in prayer with a people from a tradition quite foreign to my own. And upon arriving home, I prayed that the many divisive cultural and theological barriers which exist today might deservedly fall. I think the peyote-people, recalling my presence with them, were somewhere expressing a similar sentiment.

PART THREE

Seek and You
Will Find

*O Great Spirit, be merciful to me that my people
may live!*

—Black Elk,
"Crying for a Vision"

Whether raising a family, making a retreat, working
a shift, or embarking on a vision quest, Native thought asserts that joy and travail are the embroidery of any given
life. Time, place, and circumstance appear to be extrane-
ous to recognizing God's presence. No one is denied revelation, and, indeed, everyone is free to choose as one
pleases.

Why does one person condemn and quit the institutional Church by citing a given group's preoccupation
with fund-raising? Meanwhile, another is converted
through the example of Calcutta's self-effacing Mother
Teresa. What accounts for an individual's emphasis of
one phenomenon over the other? What influences sour or
stimulate a person's spiritual enterprise?

These are difficult questions to answer when scan-
ning crowds of Indians and non-Indians today. Soliciting
opinions would no doubt produce quite an inventory.
Among traditional Native people, however, one's reli-

gious search, or quest, was relentless. It transcended periods of weal and woe.

A common practice among most tribes consisted of one or two individuals sequestering themselves on a rise of ground nearby their encampment. This would be done on a fairly regular basis, as contact with the divine was not a taken-for-granted matter. While in isolation, strict attention was paid to all movement, all life, and any sign that could potentially reveal a supernatural message. What Christian tradition calls "discernment of spirits" is, essentially, replicated by Indian people seeking a "vision."

Once alone, however, the individual did not just passively wait for some revelation. After undergoing the sweatlodge preparation (described earlier), one would spend three or four days in complete fasting. Physical mortification during this period was often severe. After the "time-alone" period, elders would help the person interpret the meanings of this special experience. Two Leggings of the Crow tribe recounted his life-story, and his quest is representative of others.

> I walked among the . . . prairie dogs [and] I found the biggest hill . . . and dug away some earth with my knife to make a . . . resting place.
>
> The next morning I awoke to prairie dogs barking all around me . . . I found a . . . stick . . . turned toward the sun and drew out my long knife . . . and then raised my left index finger.
>
> I called the sun . . . and said that I was about to sacrifice my finger end to him. I prayed that some bird . . . or animal . . . would eat it and give me good medicine. . . .
>
> Kneeling, I placed my finger on the stick and

hacked off the end. Then I held the finger end up to the sun ... and said my prayer again. Finally I left the finger end on a buffalo chip where it would be eaten by some bird or animal.

For three days and nights I lay in that dog town, without eating or drinking....The fourth night I heard ... the words of my first medicine song ... "Anywhere you go, anywhere you go, you will be pleased."

Subsequent times in life, Two Leggings again sacrificed pieces of flesh. Such intensity might account for why some groups refer to the experience as "*crying* for a vision," although emotional, earnest, entreaties of the Supernatural are probably more to the point here. Indeed, such self-torture did not assure success. A friend of Two Leggings admitted that although he sacrificed a fingertip, nothing special was revealed. And this was not exceptional. Today, such extreme wounding is avoided.

Sometimes unsuccessful questers ritually acquired the vision power of another (a parallel to the Christian following spiritual direction?). But even if they did, persistence in finding their own was still important. Lack of success gave extra stimulus to applying oneself more assiduously. Kindred forms of repetition and mortification are, of course, not foreign to Christianity and other religious traditions. In fact, older Indians would probably commiserate with older Catholics in seeing the Friday meat-abstention lifted. Different kinds of asceticism were seen as eminently wise!

Such patient effort in the pursuit of supernatural guidance seems characteristic of traditional Indian spirituality. It echoes the encouragement of the Old Testament's Habakkuk: ". . . the vision still has its time, presses on to fulfillment, and will not disappoint. If it delays, wait for it. It will surely come; it will not be late." However, in light of modern society's high regard for efficiency, it should be apparent why such a spirituality has waned in popularity. Short-term gratifications have tended to supplant this more traditional disposition. And Indian groups have been affected by this influence as much as the dominant population.

The Sun Gives Life

The Sun, the Light of the world,
I hear Him coming,
I see His Face as He comes.
He makes the beings on earth happy,
And they rejoice.
O Wakan-Tanka, I offer to You this world of light . . .
I offer all to You.
. . .
May all be attentive and behold! . . . that they may
      live.

—Black Elk,
"The Sun Dance"

Earlier treatment of the sweatlodge ceremony and peyote ritual ought to have shown that religious questing is not just a matter of physical indifference. Characteristically, in fact, Indian spiritual practice requires a sizable investment of one's time and energy. This is manifested in another important ritual very common to widely distributed Native groupings—the "sun dance."

Reference to the ceremony as a "dance" is perhaps

somewhat misleading. The name suggests communal participation which, in reality, may or may not occur. Likewise, conventional understandings of the word "dance" suggest festivity. But too much emphasis on this element can overshadow what is primarily operative. Two Leggings is again instructive as he describes his experience of the ritual.

> ... he pinched up the skin on the right side of my chest, stuck his knife through, and inserted a wooden skewer. When he put another skewer on the left, I did not show the pain I felt. He hung a loop of buffalo rope ... over each skewer and tied the other ends to my pole.
> Crooked Arm then told me that if I felt like crying I should, but no longer than necessary. If I felt sick ... the doll ... would give me strength.
> ... I jerked ... and ... the left skewer tore loose. ... Now the right side became very painful.
> ... For the rest of that day I stood ... praying to the Great Above Person for his help in the things I would try to do.

In effect sun dance participants give powerful witness to the sincerity of their prayer. Such zeal seemed more capable of acquiring Providential aid.

Custer's Seventh Cavalry chanced upon a large encampment of Sioux and Cheyenne who were, among other activities, very likely engaged in this ritual observance. The valley of the Little Big Horn did not just contain a great number of warriors. Rather, it was the site of a community at the peak of a shared spiritual fervor. Battle figures might demonstrate that Custer was outnumbered and therefore easily defeated. But such figures fail to in-clude the inspired nature of an Indian campaign waged during so important a religious event!

Purposes for undertaking the rigors of the sun dance were (and are) many, and different groups imposed cer-tain qualifications on would-be participants. Thanksgiv-ing for prayers-answered might be the reason given by one. Another might submit to the ordeal as a penitential practice. Whatever prompted an individual to seek the honorable scarring of sun dance wounds, all considered its enactment a most sacred event.[1]

Sometimes performed in large contexts, sometimes within more private surroundings, the sun dance still re-mains an important feature of Native American religious expression. But keeping in mind that not all Indian groups maintained the observance, one should recognize the sun dance as symptomatic of a spiritual complex in North America that required far more personal invest-ment than just lip service. In this regard, it resembles the Christian proclamation that "good news" or "resurrec-tion" is an incomplete summation of faith without the doctrinal corollary of "the cross." Within Christian and Native spirituality, this "no pain—no gain" posture does not, of course, deny a spontaneous experience of the Su-pernatural. One can definitely be "knocked off one's horse" and awakened to the reality of God. The road to Damascus is well known in Native America.

Having de-emphasized the "dance" aspect of the sun ritual, attention justly ought to be refocused on it, only in

1. The blood ordeal was not an essential part of the ceremony for all tribes, while the ritual as a whole showed various forms among those groups who practiced it. Cf. Leslie Spier, *The Sun Dance of the Plains Indians: Its Development and Diffusion.* Anthropological Papers of the American Museum of Natural History, XVI, Part VII, 1921.

a broader context. Indian life today always reveals a conspicuous display of "ethnicity" through dance. Southwestern groups might calendrically stage grand exhibitions—rich in detail —which dramatize a potently operative religious heritage. These seasonal dances and festive costumes are often grounded on sacred oral traditions which have been preserved over many years. Other groups might, by contrast, be relearning ancient forms of dance which have not been vital for some time. Extended inquiry would doubtlessly reveal the spiritual foundation upon which such cultural phenomena are often built (e.g., many dances of the Great Lakes region were performed for curing the sick).

Before proceeding, however, it should be noted that "religion" and "culture" are analytical concepts. That is, they serve as abstractions that enable us to study complex realities within more manageable categories. "Culture" can refer to unconscious habitual behavior, conscious beliefs about the meaning of existence, attitudes concerning male and female roles, food, clothing, child-rearing, and everything somehow a part of a given people's way of life. Hence, students of culture generally analyze this larger framework by establishing artificial divisions. "Religion" is one of them. And this is quite understandable in light of our Western experience.

Activity for us is usually simple to define. One attends to business responsibilities during the forty-hour work-week, while religious duties (if practiced) are reserved for Sunday. Clear lines distinguish realms of "the sacred" and "the secular." In the United States particularly, this asserts itself when issues about the separation of "Church and State" arise. Americans insist that we not only avoid theocracy, but also that we somehow recognize the two as unambiguously distinct. However, as a means for analyzing culture, the term "religion" (or Church) could just as well refer to Christianity, Judaism, materialism, capitalism, or any other "guiding principle" of life. One theologian suggests that whatever is one's "ultimate concern" should be considered one's "religion"—a notion which may or may not include consideration of anything "supernatural."

Separating the different kinds of motivations which simultaneously arise within human behavior is oftentimes easier said than done. Where "politics" ends and "religion" begins is not the simple matter our Constitution would have us patriotically affirm. Such is why this profound "cultural" debate never finds closure. Even so, we still try to compartmentalize Church, state, family, work, relaxation, exercise, and other overlapping, interpenetrating realities of life. Not so for Native America!

Having outlined this problem as it exists within our own heritage, it should be apparent why Native societies present so interesting a contrast. Traditionally, they have *not* constructed boundary-lines for behavior and thought the same as we have. Indian groups did not, as a whole, discriminate between spiritual and non-religious pursuits. Dividing the two would be a meaningless fabrication because the life-cycle was perceived as a sacred, ongoing, and inter-connected process. Theoretically, at least, Christians espouse the same.

An illustration of this is the prayer reported earlier. "All are relatives" includes the capsule-testimony that everything is related and ultimately of divine origin. Thus, what we tend to view as discrete realities, Indians saw as parts of an overarching integration. And yet, because "culture" is never static, this Native worldview has undergone considerable change over the years. In many instances, the Western tendency has become the same "cultural" mode of thought among Indians (i.e., confusion).

This trend is perhaps most evident in the nationwide pageantry of ethnic "pow-wows." Throughout the year, Native groups everywhere are advertised as celebrating their tradition by inviting the public to colorful displays of feather-and-buckskin dancers. Bells jingle rhythmically as they adorn the garb of young and old. Lively movement dazzles onlookers who hear drums loudly capture the sound of quick or slow human heartbeats. Chants which accompany these different pulse-throbbings seem to express the range of human emotion. A good time appears to be had by all.

What might on the surface seem to be nothing more than a time of conviviality, visiting, and friendship is frequently at its core a religious liturgy whose sacredness was once well-known. In general, dances were named in deference to some cultural trait ("Bear," "Calumet," "Deer," "Rabbit," "Warrior," "Round," "Drum," "Scalp," etc.) that was laden with complex religious meaning. People did not just execute body movement as an arbitrary exercise of emotion. Whereas "disco" or "rock" is enjoyed by present-day Americans for social stimulation, Indian dancing has been far more circumspect. Many groups are still aware of this deeper understanding, while many are not. Nonetheless, modern pow-wows retain a communal aura that no doubt characterized more traditional, spiritually-grounded gatherings.

In my experience, two pow-wows are worth recounting here for the broader dimensions they suggest. The setting for one was a circular enclosure made of pine boughs. Under it, several hundred people reclined—leisurely contributing their necessary presence to the community-in-celebration. The circumference of the structure permitted a fairly large, open area where young and old could dance in creative unison.

Parents, grandparents, adolescents, and little-ones mingled freely under the "shade"—watching, telling funny stories, conversing seriously, playing, smiling, arranging Indian "costumes," enjoying companionship, and dramatizing, as it were, a very broad range of touching interaction. "Singers," those with the role of providing ancient chants along with their drumming, were situated in each of the cardinal directions. The tribal universe was in session. People, together, were ritually focusing their "now" with a tradition that extended beyond memory—thus rooting the present in the old and misty past. This "now" was a living out of "mythical time" which, in turn, arose from mystical timelessness—the wellspring of everything we ordinarily take for granted. Scents of evergreen filled all space with freshness.

It was announced that visitors were present whose families had long been sympathetic to Indian concerns. As it turned out, the visitors were members of a prominent eastern family that had labored on behalf of Native-rights legislation. Tradition called for an "honoring dance," and so it was begun. Shrill voices pierced the air as four drums vibrated the ground beneath. The open area was quickly filled as dancers surged rhythmically forward—a while in one direction, then back to where they started.

Seated with two elderly Indian grandmothers, I was asked to be *their* "honored guest" and join the already-in-progress dance. I was acutely self-conscious in not knowing how to perform the "steps," but these women (like grandmothers everywhere) wielded a persuasiveness that only the most hard-hearted could resist. "You'll be all right. You're with us. It's the proper thing to do"—and so I went, a reluctant grandchild, with arms clutched by two old ladies who were three times my age.

We were probably quite a sight to behold. Wrinkly-faced smiles flanked the nervous blushing of an escort that two women were either guiding or holding onto. My height rose over their frailty, as their experience masked my awkwardness. I think their smiles were the memory of long-ago dances with boys their age and a full life still ahead.

Some years have passed since that honoring time. And if pow-wows are in heaven (I suspect God stages the finest), such is what my grandmothers now enjoy forever. One of their last experiences of happy ritual and festive gathering was that moment with me.

On a later occasion, with a different tribe, I was emotionally moved by being presented with the gift of a farewell pow-wow. So that it would be a surprise, much effort was expended for everything to be "just right." Called from a previous engagement, I entered the hall and was greeted by colorfully-dressed dancers, and families that smiled happiness. All had succeeded. They had caught me off-guard.

The lead singer asked for silence and explained the purpose for gathering. We were told that an honoring dance had been requested of their "drum" (the group's generic name), and this was not a light matter. "An honoring dance is special, so we ask all to join in. Our guest will lead."

Nostalgia gripped me as I recalled the pine-boughs of an earlier place. All I could draw upon, though, was a well-practiced self-consciousness. Drums started pounding, people were getting in line, and I was alone. A tug at the sleeve broke my paralysis, and I turned to see a young child. Clad in bells and buckskin was one of the tribe's better known, though youthful, dancers. Taking my hand, we led the assembly.

Old helping young, young helping old, pow-wows, and people, and honoring the value of friendship—all filled my mind. Words spoken, rituals reinforcing them, and feelings giving substance to thought—all make the pow-wow more than just an ordinary event. While leading, I wondered if somewhere in the group a grandmother was asking for an escort. Such traditions, I realized, stretched back through generations to where the smile of God gave them birth.

Values that were forcefully alive are today more covert, as in the pow-wow context. So also, the culture/religion dichotomy, synthesized in times past, applies to many Indians as it does for other people. In fact, the social disorientation which analysts say describes Native life is no doubt greatly attributable to this rupture.

Collier's reflection quoted in the Prologue carries additional meaning in light of this problem. His "lost ingredient" seems a reference to many people's illusion that spirituality is atemporal. That is, religion for some has become a sphere of activity quite removed from life's more pressing concerns or joys. Contrasting with this, the traditional Indian world simply presents itself as comprised of people from our own continent who somehow integrated the seen and unseen, the sacred and profane, until very recent times.

In many conversations dealing with life-experiences, we frequently hear the phrase "Is that all there is?"—a phrase quite indicative of the modern mind-set. Attention is almost solely directed at surface-features which belong to the normal course of events. Traditional Indian thought has no place for such a perception. If one professes to be religious, "Is that all there is?" cannot logically be uttered. Such a person is supposed to know that living is more than a matter of organisms stimulating and responding to one another upon a field of gravity. Native religious thought coincides with Christian theologians in addressing this issue. Both recognize that nothing is ever "nothing but"; it is always "something more."

The "ingredient" appears to be the realization or awareness that life has no truly discernible beginning or end (like the often used Indian symbol, the circle). God's time-warp is infinite, and within it all creation *is*. Activity, thought, emotion, dreams, and instinct are only the palpable manifestations of existence. And today's feverish pursuit of integrity or wholeness is probably due to a felt-sense of disembodiment from this larger design, or synthesis. Individuals perceive themselves as, quite literally, individuals—as estranged chunks of humanity whose arrival and destination is of little relevance to anyone but themselves. Such is why the traditional Indian life-view is appealing. It poses an alternative to the segmentation of existence.

Television offers *Wonder Woman* and *The Six-Million-Dollar Man,* and viewers often experience heroic fantasy or a feeling that their life is not worth six cents. Although Christianity winces at these deceptions, Indians simply appear to have risen above them more adroitly.

Addressing this directly, the esteemed Black Elk is quoted as saying:

> There is much talk of peace among the Christians, yet this is just talk. Perhaps it may be, and this is my prayer, that ... peace may come to those people who can understand, an understanding which must be of the heart and not of the

head alone.... We should understand that all things are the works of the Great Spirit. We should know that He is within all things.... When we do understand all this deeply in our hearts, then we will fear, and love, and know the Great Spirit, and then we will be and act and live as He intends.

The Sacred Pipe

Mother Earth and Technology

I walk with beauty before me
I walk with beauty behind me
I walk with beauty above me
I walk with beauty below me
Beauty has been restored from the East
Beauty has been restored from the South
Beauty has been restored from the West
Beauty has been restored from the North
Beauty has been restored from the sky-top
Beauty has been restored from the earth-bottom
Beauty has been restored from all around me

—Navaho Prayer

Christ be with me
Christ within me
Christ behind me
Christ before me
Christ beside me
Christ to win me
Christ to comfort and restore me
Christ in quiet
Christ in danger

Christ in hearts of all that love me
Christ in mouth of friend and stranger
                        —St. Patrick's Breastplate

To the surprise of many easterners, vast territory
west of the Hudson River also comprises the beautiful to-
pography designated on maps as the United States. Many
are still shocked to learn that Phoenix is more than an afternoon's drive from Detroit, or that Pueblo Indians live
worlds away from New York State's Iroquoian long-
houses. The southwest's sunbaked soils paint vistas of
breathtaking beauty much different from the fertile for-
ests of the north. And seafaring folk seem quite adrift if
displaced to the rolling plains of their horseback counterparts.

Just as misconceptions have existed which lump
large regions into compact distances, so have erroneous
ideas been fostered which melt Native life into one cultural system. And yet, as muddled as this thinking has become over the years, some wisdom has survived. Indian
culture does indeed exhibit variation, but its religious
practice denotes a universal weddedness to geography's
artistic handiwork.

Whether Native homes were crafted from wigwam's
birchbark, the animal hides and wooden poles of a tepee,
igloo's snow, or southwestern soils, Indian life across the
continent was intimately associated with its regional
landscape. Necessity often required such special adaptation, but sacred myth reinforced it. Suckled with stream
water, and fed by the natural bounty of earth, Native people keenly perceived their indebtedness to the cosmos
that sustained all life. Moon's light gave assurance in the
dark, while sun's brightness shone watchfully on all

movement. Spiritual forces clearly choreographed the seasonal symphony of existence.

The vision quest, mentioned earlier, was as common to tribes of North America as this bond with the environment. In fact, the vision played a key role in people's lives because it personalized so many proximate life-forms and natural phenomena. Although one's initial, adolescent experience of the quest was generally the most profound, on many occasions throughout life an individual would seek seclusion—usually on high ground—and prayerfully implore creation's Power for aid. The panorama of the present always afforded numerous points for meditation.

In some regions, a monotheistic notion of God appears to have existed. Elsewhere, and seemingly more prevalent, the suppliant sought communication with diverse kinds of supernatural guardians. The number of such protective-generative-controlling forces varied from group to group, as did their function. All were, however, carefully identified with natural features so much a part of daily life. And even though this may sound as little more than a pantheon of spirit-entities comprising Native systems of religious thought, zealous Catholics might be reminded of their own regard for, or entreaty of, saints and angels. The truth is that something more profound seems to have been operative which neither caricature really admits. Both traditions reveal a persistent belief in the existence of a mediating, personal assistance which is supernatural, or wondrous.

Present-day Indians, perhaps from outside influence, generally express belief in a God not unlike that referred to in the Old Testament. So, too, Jesus has been widely received and is often simply called "God." Natural forces are, moreover, acknowledged as inspirational, or containing power, and individuals accord them differential respect (because they manifest "God").

Today, non-Indians are frequently indicted for not reverencing what diverse tribal folk refer to as "mother earth." Western peoples are accused of adopting a suicidal spirituality that conflicts with what might be called the Native "deposit of faith." That is, rather than preserve and protect the land on which we live—the land which gives us life—Western people are destroying it (and, ultimately, themselves). Perceiving a divine imperative in Genesis to literally "subdue the earth," non-Indians are looked upon as being prodigal children who spurn their source of life and despoil it.

Not unique to Native America, humanity's kinship to the elements is also traceable to the thought of early Greek philosophers. Predecessors of Socrates and Plato reveal in their writings a preoccupation with dissecting all life into its constitutive parts. But ancient treatises which call attention to the centrality of air, earth, fire, and water are today often seen by Americans only as quaint relics of unrefined reflection. Zoroastrianism's small Eastern following still clings to similar tenets, but Westerners often seem to dispatch such belief-systems with a condescending arrogance.

Many non-Indians seem to have transposed old reverences to the new technology—a kind of modern idol that vies for dominance with the supernatural of "less enlightened" peoples. All else is considered as primitive and unworthy of serious consideration. Yet, rather than elaborate the merits of either mind-set, it might be germane to simply highlight what has been neglected from the long and resilient tradition of Nature's pre-eminence. As the following paragraphs should illustrate, life among Native people inevitably challenges one to confront this issue.

Once the staple of many tribes, buffalo were exterminated in the name of "progress" and expansion. Then, nomadic peoples forfeited their lifestyles to salvage survival on selected tracts of land. In the words of numerous treaties, such reservations would be possessed "as long as the grass grows and river flows." However, in the name of "development," nationwide exploitation of natural resources and industrial profiteering have endangered all growing and flowing. A more subtle imperialism, this time domestic, still seems to encroach upon the Indian world.

Environmentalists warn about damage to the gene pool through nuclear and chemical poisoning, but their arguments are glibly discredited. Financially endowed self-interest groups appear to convince the multitude that "progress" will eventually calm whatever doubts may arise on this score. Meanwhile, Indian people learn of Three Mile Island and the Love Canal (two examples in a growing list), and they stoically recall annihilations suffered a century past. They painfully remember that sources which were once their livelihood did not, likewise, disappear in a day or year. Rather, disease and starvation moved almost imperceptibly through different decades and various village clusters.

Indians are made to study history so that they not "be condemned to repeat it"—as one philosopher has said. But Native America sees non-Indians voice such pedagogy in the midst of contradicting it! The destruction of natural resources proceeds just as it did in the past. And Indians ask: "Why are *we* made to study history when *you* are the ones who haven't learned?"

Native Americans, and those within their philosophical camp, see this historical process as a kind of march toward oblivion. Whereas fundamentalist Christians knock on doors asking people to admit Jesus as their "personal savior," and whereas preachers call "pagan" those who fail to embrace the Bible's literal meanings, Indians are not without reason to see Scripture itself as the harbinger of an apocalypse. How could they think otherwise?

Non-Native politicians, entrepreneurs, and bureaucrats have frequently professed a Christianity which brought holocaust to Indian America. Blind nationalism, economic gain, and environmental spoilage blend together in the minds of Native people and suggest a piety not compatible with life's most fundamental gifts—air, earth, fire, and water. Hence, the Judaeo-Christian religious convictions associated with the rise of a technological society cast little appeal. Many Indians feel that creation's most rudimentary assets have been overlooked, and their tradition maintains that such spiritual blindness can only lead to death.

Government and business leaders eye petroleum resources on foreign continents as indispensable to modern life. So, too, they command support for their claim that "national security" is at stake when access is denied. Paradoxically, a war of perhaps great magnitude is somehow perceived as insuring such access and our continued prosperity. Meanwhile, Native peoples ask why the "territorial imperative" need be so presumptuous and not be more directed at simple boundary maintenance.

Hopi elders, whose vital caution appears below, represent a spiritual mind-set American Christians might seriously heed. An essential contrast between our two "religious cultures" should be apparent.

Thoroughly acquainted with ... our religious principles ... we ... want you ... to know that we will stand firmly upon our ... religious grounds ... we will not bind ourselves to any foreign nation at this time.

Neither will we go with you on a wild and reckless adventure which we know will lead us only to a total ruin.

We have met all other rich and powerful nations who have come to our shores, from the Early Spanish Conquistadors down to the present government of the United States, all of whom have used force in trying to wipe out our existence here in our own home.

We will neither show our bows and arrows to anyone at this time. This is our only way to everlasting life and happiness. Our tradition and religious training forbid us to harm, kill and molest anyone. We, therefore, [object] to our boys being forced to be trained for war to become murderers and destroyers.

What nation who has taken up arms ever brought peace and happiness to his people?

All the laws ... of the United States were made without our consent, knowledge, and approval, yet we are being forced to do everything that we know is contrary to our religious principles and those principles of the Constitution.

Now we ask you, American people, what has become of your religion and your tradition? Where
do we stand today? The time has come now for all
of us ... to re-examine ourselves, our past deeds,
and our future plans. The judgment day will soon
be upon us. Let us make haste and set our house
in order before it is too late.

This is our sacred duty to our people.

These Hopi words may sound in the 1980's as a timely
statement relative to prevailing crises, and yet they were
pleaded over thirty years ago! Regardless of arguments
voiced on behalf of Christian "defense" or aggression,
such Native groups repeatedly offer the above worldview
as an alternative. Non-Indians might express similar aspirations, but why have Native people been the only ones
to achieve them?

Francis of Assisi, a Catholic saint and founder of the
Franciscan Order, personified nature in a prayer which
strongly evokes Native concepts. His "Canticle of Brother
Sun" is probably closer to Indian religious sentiment than
many of the more scholarly reconstructions. A "classic"
of the Christian prayer-tradition, the Canticle is a fitting
capstone to what the Hopi and other groups have repeatedly suggested.

... Be praised, my Lord, for all Your creatures.
In the first place for the blessed Brother Sun,
Who gives us the day and enlightens us through
    You.
He is beautiful and radiant with his great splendor,
Giving witness of You, Most Omnipotent One.

Be praised, my Lord, for Sister Moon and the stars
Formed by You so bright, precious, and beautiful.

Be praised, my Lord, for Brother Wind
And the airy skies, so cloudy and serene;
For every weather, be praised, for it is life-giving.

Be praised, my Lord, for Sister Water,
So necessary yet so humble, precious and chaste.

Be praised, my Lord, for Brother Fire,
Who lights up the night.
He is beautiful and carefree, robust and fierce.

Be praised, my Lord, for our sister, Mother Earth,
Who nourishes and watches us
While bringing forth abundance of fruits with
    colored flowers
And herbs . . .

Be praised, my Lord, for those who pardon through
    Your love
And bear weakness and trial.
Blessed are those who endure in peace,
For they will be crowned by you, Most High.

Be praised, my Lord, for our sister, Bodily Death,
Whom no living man can escape.
Woe to those who die in sin.
Blessed are those who discover the holy will.
The second death will do them no harm.

Praise and bless my Lord.
Render thanks.
Serve Him with great humility.

A God for All Seasons

"Married yet?"

"Gonna get married next year."

"... where are you staying?"

"Her dad's place. But them people say we got to get our own relief."

... What do you say, Arne Saunders, you who would get a job ... and build a cabin out of the timber that stands there ... for the taking, if it was you/but/if you were Jacob it would all be hopeless or something else so inexplicably different from what it would be for you that you cannot guess at it ...

" ... have you tried to get a job?"

"I can't get no job."

... Arne imagined how it was in the hiring office; the expressionless face and the cheap teenage clothing ... all these taken in ... and the stock answer given coldly, nothing just now, maybe in a month or so.

... Arne Saunders, what do you know of that, you who could have turned up the palms of your hands when you were fifteen and shown callouses ... what, really, can you know?

"Janet going to have a baby?"

"Pretty quick I guess."

... Arne ... went on thinking about a young couple starting married life in a corner of the old people's place which was ... where most married life in Kwatsi did start ...

"When you gonna build me a house?"

"We said it would take time and new families have formed... faster than we can keep up."

"What d'ya have to do?"

". . . when your band council decides you're next for help."

"They ain't gonna do nothin' for me. . . . When do I get some relief?"

Jacob left the car and Arne watched him slouch along toward his in-laws.

Jacob, you have just taken the last shred of fight out of me but you, you poor bastard, never had any to start with.

You're nineteen and you're dead already.

—Alan Fry,
How a People Die

Visiting New Mexico's Acoma pueblo required turning off the smooth interstate highway and slowly bumping over dirt roads which led to its path of ascent. Had not a film company built the town's only access route, it would have been necessary to climb time-worn rockways. A centuries-old village of adobe silently accepted my arrival.

High above the windswept terrain, Acoma reveals itself as a sentinel of the desert. Uninterrupted natural beauty gleams in every direction as each eye-blink photographs indelible memories. Air's freshness is scented with unknown perfumes of the earth, and dizziness is prevented by finally recognizing the need to exhale. Wrinkled faces watched quietly and smiled knowingly at my initiation.

Dome-shaped, outdoor ovens, religious ceremonial centers called "kivas," small homes, and a Catholic church were all cleanly made from soils of the surrounding countryside. The "Enchanted Mesa," an uninhabited and inaccessible rise of land several miles distant, seemed to look at Acoma's design approvingly. Earth and life-forces merged in the observable panorama of existence. They called one's interior caravan of questions to calm. Something was there.

Several hours later, en route to California and alertly watching for the desert's road-scurrying creatures, I was shocked into the neon reality of Las Vegas. My previously uninterrupted awe of nature was broken by a cacophony of diffuse sounds. They filled the atmosphere and back-dropped scenes of hustling-bustling "back home" folk who mixed about with street-wise professionals.

Faces varied. Some appeared hopeful of winning long-sought fortunes. Others seemed desperate, as if banished from an Eden they once took for granted. All human activity was counter-pointed by the constant movement of spinning wheels, and the alluring, tired arms of greedy slot-machines.

Such motion, such life, such color, such light—at three o'clock in the morning. In many places, musicians with expressionless faces played rote tunes as singers echoed popular radio hits. Drinking fountains stood unused and dry, as thirsts were quenched by some kind of alcoholic beverage clasped in seemingly every hand.

Acoma's still beauty came to mind—so integrated and harmonious with the afternoon's natural splendor. Its memory clashed violently with the manufactured glow and transitory actions of everything I beheld. Its serenity was replaced with nervous unrest. Its year-round occupants were far removed from the uprooted people I beheld. Unlike Acoma, people here did not seem content to be quietly by themselves. They were, rather, entranced by the promises of untrustworthy casino ads. Something was missing.

Driving away, I was flagged down by a scantily-clad

Indian woman no more than twenty years old. Penniless and hungry, she asked for enough money to buy a meal and perhaps a "drink." She offered to work for the handout if need be. I said she would not have to earn anything, and that we could simply talk. We drove to a restaurant.

Between the several servings she swiftly consumed, I was able to hear of her "life ambition." Unlike the "vision quest" so hallowed in her tribe's earlier religious tradition, the goal she sought had no purposeful contribution in focus. Feeling relaxed, her appetite sated, she became serious and confided: "I want to go to Hollywood and become a star." Her statement was pitiful because of its unreality. Apart from having no preparation for such a dream, disease-scars crossed a perhaps once pretty face, and social skills were quite a few years shy of what I knew to be average for her age. And yet, maybe this unfulfilled wish kept her alive.

Asking why she had left her family, I was informed that Indian life had no future. "Indians never make any progress. Besides, there's no action back home like there will be in Hollywood." Leaving her at the restaurant door, I wished her well.

I was reminded of how many non-Indians had similarly indicted their families and traditions. How many had abandoned their homes, and pursued illusions of strength outside an enduring and life-giving religious heritage? Whether Indian or not, people just seem to be tantalized by fashionable trends which, in the long run, often only broaden one's interior void. A more potent experience of "now" repeatedly presents itself as existing on the next mesa, or in the next city or spiritual tradition. Witnessing this pattern so frequently among so many diverse persons, I found myself nodding to the insight of Greek, Christian, Zoroastrian, and Native American sages. It seemed to have been lost in the fast pace of a more "sophisticated" society.

In essence, it claims the Divine is as near as the air we breathe. God is the earth-like foundation upon which all activity rests. The Supernatural quickens our pulse and kindles the flame-like quality of our human spirit. The Power of creation is the quenching hope we can somehow still retain during life's more drying times. Air, earth, fire, and water suddenly seemed as a kind of natural Eucharist—the nourishing recognition that all belongs to God, and that the handiwork of creation broadcasts the majesty of just being alive. Whatever Ultimate Source claimed responsibility for existence within differing religious traditions, accord was unanimous that one's search for substance, or purpose, or fulfillment could be found in the immediate landscape of each individual. One's moment of discovery is always at hand.

Within the Native mind, elements like air, earth, fire, and water conspire to remind one of the circumventing reality of God. By contrast, the non-Indian stewardship of resources presents itself as an abomination of Native religion's most fundamental tenet. Indestructible nuclear pollutants, poisoned water, choking air, and farmland filled with asphalt become more than just unfortunate by-products of economic growth. They suggest to Native America that Western society is a cancerous force bent on actively overcoming the Supernatural. "Progress" and technology are perceived as simply having abused nature too often. Such overkill might be compared to, as one tribal group says, "laughing at butterflies." This is unacceptable. It is not done. Hence, the conflict of ideology is a non-negotiable one. Life and death are at stake.

The Appendix gives some indication of the extent to which Native America relied on the environment for, among other things, the restoration of health. The list of flora that were commonly used could be expanded several times over. What we often consider to be just weeds or simple field-flowers and plants were trustworthy "friends" to Indian people across the continent. Their indiscriminate elimination by a world that aborts them at will can only terrorize a people whose tradition they sustained.

Although Christianity represents no contradiction to the spirit of this traditional Indian sentiment, too many Christians have. In this way, Native America challenges these Gospel adherents to re-evaluate their perhaps nominal commitment. The angry words of a once-Christian Indian activist reflect the disaffection created by years of culture-contact: "The only person to ever really live Christianity was Jesus, and you killed him. So don't tell us anymore about following your religion!" Not just a reference to the historical fact, his words indict a belief-system that often remains more theory than practice.

The Dormitory of Life

"Father, Great Spirit, help my people and all things to live in a sacred manner. May our people always send their voices to You as they walk the sacred path of life."

—Black Elk

While an instructor at Red Cloud Indian School, I was also involved with taking care of a dormitory which housed the high school boys. Forty or so young men, between the ages of thirteen and twenty, were housed in a large room filled with bunk-beds. Nightly, "lights out" occurred at 10:30. This was preceded by an hour of "winding down" that often amounted to little more than organized bedlam. In the course of a given evening, we would supervise the dorm and face situations that were sometimes challenging, sometimes inspiring.

I might be playing checkers with a freshman and then be called to cool tempers that were flaring between a couple of seniors. A short distance from this, a junior might be already in bed, just looking upward, obviously in need of parent-like presence. Words would be exchanged, and maybe the young man would fall to sleep knowing someone cared. On occasion, one of the boys might even whisper: "Tuck me in." Regularly, one or two would need a reprimand for using our living-area as a basketball court. Many of these young people had life-experiences far beyond their years.

A good number of our dorm group now have families of their own. Perhaps they raise their children and recall with some warmth the parenting they knew in the dormitory. Apart from carrying gratitude to have lived with such rich personalities, I know I am indebted to them for what they showed me concerning prayer.

When lights were extinguished and I or another moved to the center of the dorm, all we had to utter was: "Okay, guys, let's say a prayer." No matter what comments were in progress, or what clowning still active, the announced moment of prayer would usher in a silent stillness. Fifty people would suddenly be hushed as the dormitorian would pray on behalf of everyone present.

A typical prayer might be like the following: "Grandfather, Great Spirit, Father in heaven, thank you for this day. Thank you for the people who were part of our day. Guide our families, and teach us how to love as Jesus did—especially when it's difficult. Protect those who have

108 THE SACRED VISION

no bed to sleep in this night. Waken us tomorrow with hope, and bless us with the gift of a new day. Amen." Our last words would always be "Good night, guys"—and from various places in the dark, voices would wish us the same.

The formative years of many present-day reservation leaders have included this nightly routine. And although circumstances have changed, it was always apparent that we were simply continuing a time-honored tradition that pre-dated cars and schools, bunk-beds and basketball.

Museum-like, the reservation records a century of social upheaval. As with other parts of Indian country, there still lived people whose childhood was in a different age. Younger generations might pass them on a highway, only to read about their grandparents in textbooks dealing with "the Old West." A chronicle of wearing apparel, from buckskin to designer jeans, would mark the different age-groups. But more importantly, this array of fashion gave partial witness to a religious truth that young ones instinctively preserved. All things have their time and pass. Clothing-styles may change, but human dependence on God does not.

Social conditions fluctuate over the decades, and "creature-comforts" become little more than temporary fads. However, misfortune and gladness are not prejudiced. They entwine each life. Aware of all this, our dormitory youth would finish their day—knowing of life's only enduring necessity.

Praying made sense. How else could one hope to achieve right conduct? How else could one find meaning to life?

Indian elders passed on to their young a sustaining wisdom of long-standing years. Relating to God exposes phantoms of dread. Nightmares of life are thus chased away so that one can dream of tomorrow.

The Journey to Forever

Death like life is a mystery and must have its origin and meaning. Both are natural, but in naming them "natural" merely their fact is stated; neither is explained. They are interbound in meaning . . . for First Things and Last Things are of one creation, and cosmogony and eschatology are but the beginning and ending of a single narrative.

—Hartley Burr Alexander,
The World's Rim

"Happy hunting ground" is the stereotyped reference to an afterlife that many people associate with Native America. It does not, however, do justice to the many notions that Indian groups actually possessed. How could Native fishermen or agriculturalists consider it a reward to spend eternity chasing game-animals? Would such a "heaven" require the harsh demands of maintaining a subsistence pattern? Or does the notion imply that well-fed animals would surrender themselves to a camp and mysteriously be rendered edible without the time-consuming preparation?

A form of the concept certainly applied to some hunter-groups, but to others it was foreign (even though they might discuss it as an interesting thought). In times past, ideas about what occurred at death varied from region to region. Yet, these different understandings have been greatly affected by centuries of exposure to outside influences. Today, some kind of life-after-life, or heaven, has become part of the Indian religious heritage.

While varied wake and burial ceremonies offer much for reflection, what I shall call "cemetery-reverence" will be described here. This widespread phenomenon essentially consists of a community's orchestration of prayer, song, grave-maintenance, visiting, and a "feed." Some groups perform this observance just once a year. Others will congregate more often (with different embellishments for each occasion).

Not just a simple recasting of Memorial Day, this behavioral complex hints of ancient traditions known to pre-history. Archaeologists excavate North America's many burial mounds and try to interpret the cultural systems which motivated their construction. Quite often, their explanations conflict. Were researchers to participate in present-day cemetery rituals, they might better comprehend the spirit which animated mound-builders of centuries earlier.

Browsing through old photographs from Native collections, I frequently wondered why the different groups expended so much energy on communal processions. Turn-of-the-century shots show elders and babes captured by celluloid from one moment in time. Faces smile, look back, or glance away. Some appear self-conscious. Some are not aware of being so caught by the open shutter. Others seem to be issuing a reprimand—as if to say that my inquisitive gaze has lasted too long. I often wondered if some of the people in these pictures were still living. Maybe some of the small children still survived. Questions would come to mind and remain unanswered: Why did you gather like this? What were you thinking? Who organized your gathering?

The still-figures of faded, greyish-white photographs could not respond, but answers were forthcoming. Dull prints were transformed into vivid impressions when I attended a cemetery observance in northern Ontario. It was late summer among the Ojibwa, and rainbow-colored leaves silently broadcast the passing of warm days.

A small wooden church was where the event would begin at noon. Near this structure, drivers had deserted their new or dilapidated cars and trucks. It seemed as if an insoluble maze of metal knots flanked, armor-like, the people's place of prayer.

Perhaps the configuration was symbolic—a kind of distancing of the secular from the sacred, the earthworks of old replaced by a novel use of modern horsepower. Or was this a kind of deferential gesture to the children at play? I watched their dark eyes gleam as sunshine glistened heads of jet-black hair. Squeals of giggling laughter refreshed my memory that one of childhood's greatest delights was to be chased around immovable objects.

To these little ones, the disarray of cars and trucks was a playground of engineering triumph. It provided the thrilling challenge of eluding bullies, discovering hidden playmates, and vocalizing new sounds never before heard! Emma bumped heads with Marie near the van. Emil caught Matthew behind the Ford. I realized then how a city's manicured, partitioned parking lot seemed so inconsiderate of young bodies. Such were my thoughts as the scene unfolded before me. Leaving one's car as part of this confusion revealed itself as a first stage of the ritual, so there I parked. With two smiling, golden faces peeking through my window, I felt I had somehow made a small contribution to the day's happiness.

Hymns (some in Ojibwa) signaled everyone to gather. Colorful banners fluttered in the breeze as proud bearers held long lances high. A Catholic priest, fully-vested, carried a consecrated Communion wafer. He was escorted by four men of the community who bore a canopy. Prayers were begun inside the church, and silence fell upon the gathering who, by now, were spilling out into an open area of windswept grass. The young had abandoned their motionless playground and could be seen interspersed with mothers and fathers, grandparents and young adults. Special time—time set apart, sacred time—was being observed.

Upon completing a number of intercessory prayers, the priest was slowly led toward the village cemetery. It was a parcel of land beyond the tree-line. Joining the procession was anyone who could manage the distance of just over a mile. With several others, I stopped to hug Mary Morningstar—aged matriarch of the community who insisted upon being brought to the event despite her bedridden condition. Tears dropped from her eyes as we acknowledged her welcome presence. It was clear that she took joy in being able to come, even though her ascent to the graves would have to occur another, perhaps final, time. Mary had faithfully participated in this ceremony for over eighty years.

The group's composition, and the path itself, combined to form a lasting image. All ages were represented, and were mixed together. Parts of the road were steep and rocky, and some people needed support. Some stretches were smooth and flat. They offered relief to grandparents whose canes were of little help earlier on.

The pace was slow and solemn while religious songs counterpointed periods of silent meditation. Children dutifully trailed behind elders, and some people just walked by themselves in quiet contemplation. Several leaders repeatedly tried to get the column to sing, but not everyone

knew the verses. Along the way, some younger men discussed business matters. Still, they plodded on with older
folk who seemed to have a more reverential bearing. As
we neared the cemetery ridge, I paused to look back at
those struggling on. It was then that I perceived the
event's deeper meaning.

Census-takers could have saved themselves much effort by attending this activity. The whole community
filled the road—the priest and his attendants now in the
cemetery-village at one end, Mary Morningstar and her
nurses near the church at the other. Between these two
figures, a people journeyed—the young and old, the
healthy and infirm, leaders, listeners, contemplatives,
and the preoccupied. But the social status that someone
held in life was only temporary, as all shared the common destiny of the grave. Regardless of varied tempera-
ments and abilities, death was the sobering equalizer of
humanity. And the cemetery-reverence ritualized this reality. One's presence, translated, meant: "We need to be
reminded of this."

Some arrived at the ridgetop before others, but eventually the entire column was gathered among the plots.
Indeed, we were creating, in anticipatory fashion, what
would someday come to pass. The mood was more medi-
tative than somber—the experience eliciting a consideration of life itself.

So there we all stood—a group of human beings upon
soil that would one day be on us. No one seemed to mind
the physical closeness that gradually developed. Young
arms reached around adult waists. Wrinkled hands
clutched grandchildren. And those who normally steered
away from each other in the daily routine now allowed,
truce-like, a shoulder-to-shoulder nearness.

The priest began to pray, and visitors started to take

snapshots. I noticed that some of the people would smile at the photographer. Some looked the other way. Some seemed uncomfortable, as they perhaps regarded picture-taking a discourteous thing to do at such a time.

Before the priest and his attendants started downhill, time was permitted for people to take care of their family plots. Once the procession resumed, our journey back to the church was the same as during ascent. The "circle" was complete—ending where it had begun.

The dinner that followed was a capstone to the day's activity. Good will permeated the Ojibwa community. All had once again affirmed their continuity with generations past and generations of the now. Their admission that all comes from, and returns to, God was evident. Even the ever-present household dogs deserved a few choice table-scraps on this occasion.

A relaxed calm was appropriate now, for it was very good belonging to such a group. And it was very good to settle back and watch the younger people take such joy in playing around the parked cars. I sat with proud elders who knew that this tradition would be carried on by the youth. And we smiled at their play.

It was evening, and I noticed Emil catching Matthew behind the Ford. And not far from them, Marie bumped heads with Emma.

Nature and Institutional Religious Practice

Like two cathedral towers these stately pines
Uplift their fretted summits tipped with cones;
The arch beneath them is not built with stones,
Not Art but Nature traced those lovely lines,

And carved this graceful arabesque of vines;
No organ but the wind here sighs and moans,
No sepulchre conceals a martyr's bones,
No marble bishop on his tomb reclines.

Enter! the pavement, carpeted with leaves,
Gives back a softened echo to thy tread!
Listen! the choir is singing; all the birds,

In leafy galleries beneath the eaves,
Are singing! listen, ere the sound be fled
And learn there may be worship without words.

—Henry Wadsworth Longfellow[2]
"My Cathedral"

Besides giving us memorable verse, Longfellow has also bequeathed a legacy of American place-names second only to the Bible. But apart from this curious geographical fact, the poet's influence on our concept of Native spirituality seems just as pervasive. Inspired by Schoolcraft's memoirs from the Great Lakes region, Longfellow masterfully penned what he imagined to be a natural religion.

Weaned on the shining waters of "Gitchee Gumee" (Lake Superior), and raised in cathedrals of pine (the north woods), Native people knew, felt, and breathed the earthiest elements born of a Creator. In fact, so Longfellow would reason, this union mystically bridged the seen and unseen, matter and spirit, person and God. A fuller humanity seemed more apparent here, and Western cul-

2. Quoted from Anita Dore, ed., *The Premier Book of Major Poets*, Fawcett Publications Inc., Greenwich, Conn., 1970, p. 181.

tures had somehow lost this primal bond. Perhaps they never possessed it. Whatever the truth, this special commodity is observably sought today ("natural food" stores and restaurants are part of this trend). Many school children have inherited Longfellow's thought and have made it their own.

Reflections of this nature come to mind as I look out over the lake made famous by the poet. Its temperamental waters had recently sunk the Edmund Fitzgerald. Now they show themselves as an inviting pool of blue.

Down the coast to my right are empty resort cabins. Their summertime owners make winter hibernation in the thickets of city convenience. To my left and behind me are the year-round dwellings of reservation Chippewa. Their Canadian cousins have homes which line the opposite shore, mirror-like, across the bay. Up the road is the site of an old beachfront battleground. An Iroquois war-party was destroyed there by Michigan Indians who had grown weary of their incursions. Never again were the Iroquois tempted to paddle this far into Lake Superior, but invasions of a different kind still occur.

City-people often seek relief in this wilderness hideaway. They find here a refreshing contrast to their normal routine—synthetic worlds of wholly human design. Interestingly, some theologians have likened the American posture toward God in these very images. That is, people are sometimes controlled by notions of a deity who is undiscriminating, permissive, accepting, and coddling. This is the God associated with rural settings. At other times, people feel manipulated, punished, disliked, or cajoled. The association here is with a God of things urban. Within these opposite settings, it is suggested, people formulate concepts of the Divine. Consequently, doctrinal differences may not entirely account for why non-Indians turn for spiritual direction from Native America. Instead, confusion might be arising from a culture that perpetrates a kind of spiritual subterfuge.

On the other hand, generations of city-bred Indians, quite removed from their ethnic tradition, have also joined this search. Decades (or even centuries) of moving and intermarriage have obscured the reasons why they first parted from tribal ways. But one strongly felt experience remains. Whether buffeted too long by ghetto poverty, or no longer enamored with the white man's shiny creations, they pray that an alternative lifestyle exists. Religious sentiment, per se, might initially have no role in this re-evaluation. Modern America is somehow found wanting, then, by both non-Indians and Native people. Their pursuit of a "better life" emerges from a shared disillusionment with what the Western world offers.

Ironically, however, reservations also see their young depart! People move to the cities and, echoing those they pass along the way, claim that "something more" is surely to be had elsewhere. One reason this occurs is that Arctic Eskimo, coastal fishermen, desert dwellers, and isolated others are not immune from media influence. Daily telecasts convince some people that real living remains outside their wilderness borders. Native rituals, if at all practiced, are judged out-of-step with twentieth century life. What some value as solitude, others perceive as boredom. This slow lifestyle is exchanged for the faster pace of swollen cities. Grocery stores present a welcome respite from having to harvest one's own food. And sacred myths which the elders preserve are deemed fairly irrelevant to enterprising youth.

In the midst of these comings and goings, others remain where they are and retain a spirituality that bars rigid definition. Whether Native or Christian, rural or urban, Indian religious constructs are intact. They provide an integration that many fail to appreciate or achieve for themselves. What goes into creating this division (sometimes within a single family) is difficult to name. Watching these social dynamics, these vision-seeking people, and vision-found folk, one is acutely confronted with the stressful reality that religious journeys can include.

Non-Indians frequently renounce various expressions of Christianity and orient their spiritual concerns in the direction of something more "natural." Indians often make similar repudiations. Some from these groups voice vague aspirations and some seem to confuse religious experience with cultural disaffection. Others, however, represent a block of questions that Christian thinkers need to seriously address.

Where has the Gospel message been distorted? How have Scripture-based people not convincingly lived their belief? What in Native practice has been too readily overlooked or dismissed? Why are the two traditions popularly regarded as antithetical if, in fact, the same God revealed them? Perhaps some answers may be fleshed out more easily than others. Unfortunately, some people remain living aloof from both the questions and the answers.

Indian religious practice described here in Part Three has been, unlike the pipe and peyote sections, concentrated and kaleidoscopic. The intention of these vignette-experiences is to demonstrate the spirit which underlies more thorough analyses of the Indian religious spectrum.

One of the prevailing themes worthy of attention is religious consciousness itself. As mentioned earlier, Native people are (like non-Indians) sometimes not very familiar with their own tradition. At other times, their knowledge is reflexive and implicit. By contrast, religious specialists who devote their time to such thought are more articulate. But this is not unique. Some years ago, anthropologist Paul Radin noted that this pattern of consciousness and articulation surfaced in all cultures. If such is the case, religious experience poses a significant, personal challenge. Posed as a question, it might read: "How serious and sincere am I in seeking the truth about life?" An honest answer to this might be the necessary first-phase in spiritual growth. Liberation can then be felt as horizons, formerly hidden, bring light.

As with many non-Indians, some people might sound better than their relationships affirm. More than a case of "actions speaking louder than words," their behavior jeopardizes the usefulness or integrity of whatever creed is professed. By their fruits we might know individuals, but unfortunately we remain ignorant of the spirituality they sorely misrepresent. And so, violations of what is outlined here are easily found—as among any community.

Accepting that world religions are the heritage of humanity (and not restricted to an exclusive genetic group), one should be quite capable of appropriating religious insights wherever they can be found. Indeed, if an avenue to God is opened this way, both Christianity and Native spirituality would encourage its pursuit. Both traditions agree that in life nothing matters except trying to find God until no more time is left to search.

EPILOGUE

"My heart shakes hands with yours."
                              —Lakota greeting

These pages have not exhausted all the dimensions of
Native spirituality. No book of a leisurely readable length
could do so. Rather, they have simply attempted to highlight time-honored traditions and impulses still alive today.

What would, in the modern era, be considered peculiar or bizarre aspects of the past have been avoided, as
such aspects of Indian tradition would serve more to dis-
tract than to diagnose. Coverage of things like cannibal-
ism, human sacrifice, or scalping would probably cause
readers to perpetuate long-standing ethnocentric notions
of barbarism that should best be laid to rest. Oddities of
this nature could be easily enough put into context and
understood, but digressing on them rightly belongs to anthropological analysis. Instead, these pages have addressed what *now* exists in Native America.

By the same token, such concepts as the Navahoan
hozhq have also been de-emphasized. For example, *hozhq*
implies the fullness of being—harmony, integration, long
life, beauty, and so forth. Dwelling too much on how a

people conceives of the ideal might run the risk of doing what some Christian tracts have done, allowing readers to get pretty discouraged by comparing their felt-frailty with religious formulations of what constitutes a kind of "sinless state." The real-life experience of communicating with God includes wrestling at times (as with the Old Testament's Jacob), and perhaps this would be missed through such a portrayal. If anything has been thematic in these pages, it has been a certain Native perseverance in religious questing—in bad times and good.

As has also been evident, Indian conceptions of God or the supernatural have not remained in their "pure form" over the years. Indian people have not sat idly by and let Christianity escape their notice. Interestingly, too, some who are regarded as old-time practitioners (or even anti-Christian) actually profess belief in a system greatly influenced by three centuries of contact. Hence, any treatment of contemporary Native religious practice would not be accurate unless this was underscored. It should even be noted that most Indian people are not active in traditional forms. Those who do participate in religion frequently affiliate with Christian Churches.

This work has attempted to describe identifiable themes that have persisted. Should some of this essay's reflections sound too intellectualized or, by contrast, overly romantic, such seems to be the extremes that bound religious experience itself. The English poet Wordsworth wrote that we could never prove the existence of immortality—only struggle for "intimations" of it. Perhaps one's search for God entails a similar process. Maybe any attempt to impart "belief" can only be suggestive, or impressionistic, and thus struggle with disparate forms of articulation. Such has been the range of this book.

Native America has aided my religious quest and,

somewhat like the evangelists, I have written about Indian religious practices I consider most telling. As with the Gospels, whatever I report cannot be coercive. If the faith of some readers has been buttressed, or if a greater understanding of Indian religion has been communicated, then this work has been worth the effort. If one seeks to know more about Native or Christian practice, I heartily encourage further investigation. To quote, more or less, the final lines of St. John: if Indian or Christian spirituality was written about in detail, I doubt that there would be room enough in the entire world to hold the books to record it.

APPENDIX

A Sample of Plant Uses in Native North America

Plant Name	Used For
Alder	Diseases of the eye
Alum-root	Teething; dysentery; diseases of the eye
Anemone	Wounds; eyes; sores
Arbor vitae	Kidney trouble
Balsam Fir	Rheumatism
Black Rattle-Pod	Rheumatism
Blackberry	Lung trouble
Blue Cohosh	Fever
Blue Flag	Swelling; earache; sores; eyes; bruises
Britton	Dysentery
Buroak	Cramps
Burdock	Pleurisy; coughing
Burning Brush	Uterine trouble
Bush Morning-Glory	Used to stop anxiety and bad dreams
Butterfly Weed	Heart; bronchial; sores
Calamus	Sore throat; stomach trouble; inflammation and troubled skin; ulcers
Cardinal Flower	Love charm
Carrion-flower	Pain in the back; kidney trouble
Catnip	Fever
Cat-tail	Chafing

Choke Cherry	Diarrhea
Coral Berry	Weak or inflamed eyes
Cow Parsnip	Fainting; convulsions; pain; boils
Culver's Root	Cleansed the blood
Cup-Plant	Bathing
Fetid Marigold	Headache
Fuzzy-Weed	Love and hunting charm
Giant Hyssop	An internal cold with tendency to pneumonia; also pain in chest; indigestion
Goldenrod	Used for burns; pain in the back; lung trouble; sprains; remedies for the hair; boils; enemas
Greene	Fever
Hops	Fever; intestinal pains
Ironwood	Kidney trouble
Jack-in-the-Pulpit	Fever; toothache; cough
Jacob's Ladder	Hoarseness
Joe-Pye Weed	Helps a child to go to sleep
Ladyslipper	Toothache; inflammation of skin; stomach trouble
Land Plant	Neuralgia; rheumatism
Lily	Bites of poisonous reptiles
Little Wild Sage	Irregular menstruation
Lodgepole Pine	Coughs
Long-Fruited Anemone	Good luck
Loveseed	Love charm
Meadow Rue	Fragrance; love potion; stimulant
Milkweed	Lactations; dysentery
Tall Milkweed	Stomach ache

Mountain Mint	Stoppage of periods
Mugwort	Dysentery; diseases of women; hemorrhages; remedies for the hair
Narrow-Leaved Purple Cone	Snake bite; headache; burns
Pasque Flower	Rheumatism
Pilot Weed	Chewing gum
Plantain	Charm; rheumatism; bites
Prairie Ground Cherry	Headache; stomach trouble
Purple Mallow	Head cold; internal pains
Ragweed	Nausea
Red Brush	Smoking
Red False Mallow	Salve for burns
Red Oak	Bowels
Red Raspberry	Cataract
Red Root	Tea; fuel
Red Stick	Smoking
Shadbush	Given to a pregnant woman who has been injured to prevent miscarriage
Shepherd's Purse	Cramps
Soapweed	Soap
Sour Dock	Diarrhea
Spider-Bean	Itching
Squirrel-tail	Sty; inflammation of lid
Sumac	Teething; dysentery
Sweet Cicely	Ulcers; used to stop weakness
Sweet Grass	Perfume
Sunflower	Heart trouble
White Pine	Cuts
Wild Bergamot	Facial blemishes

Wild Black Currant	Kidney; uterus
Wild Cherry	Worms; ulcers; disinfectant wash
Wild Columbia	Fragrance; love charm; fever; headache
Wild Four-o-clock	Fever; swelling; sore mouth
Wild Fox-glove	Chills; fever
Wild Ginger	Indigestion
Wild Licorice	Toothache; earache; fever
Wild Lettuce	Warts
Wild Plum	Abrasions
Wild Rose	Cataracts; burns; eyes
Wild Sage	Bathing
Wild Touch-me-not	Rash; eczema
Wild Verbena	Stomach ache
Yarrow	Earache

A Selective Bibliography

Alexander, Hartley Burr, *The World's Rim: Great Mysteries of the North American Indians.* Lincoln: University of Nebraska Press, 1953.

Brown, Joseph Epes, *The Sacred Pipe: Black Elk's Account of the Seven Rites of the Oglala Sioux.* Norman: University of Oklahoma Press, 1953.

Collier, John, *Indians of the Americas.* New York: Mentor Books, 1947.

Craven, Margaret, *I Heard the Owl Call My Name.* New York: Dell Publishing Co., 1973.

Deloria, Vine, *God Is Red.* New York: Grosset & Dunlap, 1973.

Driver, Harold E., *Indians of North America.* Chicago: University of Chicago Press, 1961.

Fry, Alan, *How a People Die.* New York: Tower Publications, 1970.

La Barre, Weston, *The Peyote Cult.* New York: Schocken Books, 1969.

Nabokov, Peter, *Two Leggings: The Making of a Crow Warrior.* New York: Thomas Y. Crowell Company, 1967.

Ortiz, Alfonso, *The Tewa World: Space, Time, Being and Becoming in a Pueblo Society.* Chicago: University of Chicago Press, 1969.

Starkloff, Carl F., *The People of the Center: American Indian Religion and Christianity.* New York: The Seabury Press, 1974.

Underhill, Ruth M., *Red Man's Religion.* Chicago: University of Chicago Press, 1965.

Witherspoon, Gary, *Language and Art in the Navajo Universe.* Ann Arbor: University of Michigan Press, 1977.